Joanne —
This is to favorite peop[le]
Thanks for always be[ing]
wonderful to be with. I love you so much. Your grandfather helped make both of us who we are today.

Jim —
Thanks for being the guy that gets to take care of Joanne — that important task couldn't be in better hands.

I love you both
Cousin
Mike
2013

"*The Book of Testosterone* covers a lot of what I've learned from my best teammates. Thank God he left out the part about cannibalism."
—Terry Whelan, former player for the
United States National Rugby Team

"When I first started hunting with Mike, he put me into one of his deer stands ... within an hour I took a beautiful 8-point buck. I've been listening to his advice ever since."
—Captain Michael Ireland (USN Retired)

"Seldom Wrong, Never in Doubt ... that's *The Book of Testosterone* ... my newest reference manual."
—Bob Herron, Famous Brother
President, Mediaworks Pro Group

"I truly loved *The Book of Testosterone* ... I know it is going to improve my bar act."
—Dave Hamberg, Bon Vivant and Raconteur
President, Paladin Funding Corporation

"There's never been a better time in history to man-up. Mike has given us wisdom for millions of sons from hundreds of fathers ... insight that can be a guiding force in any man's life."
—John Carr, Chairman and CEO,
Brain Surgery Worldwide, Inc.

"Next time you need a shot of gumption, pick up Mike's book—and a beer!"
>—Porter Hardy, President
>Smartmouth Brewing Co.

"What a great read. Once I started I couldn't put it down. Now I know who the saying 'Be Like Mike' is really about. One is never too old to get a reminder on what it takes to be a man."
>—Brian Vizard, Executive Director
>United States Rugby Football Foundation
>Former Captain, United States National
>Rugby Team

"As a surgeon, I've had the pleasure of putting Mike back together on several occasions; first the left shoulder, then the right shoulder, then re-attaching a bicep, and then fixing one of his knees ... you wouldn't believe the scar tissue in this man ... but after reading his book, I just wish we were fishing together more often!"
>—Dr. Raymond Payne, M.D.
>Atlantic Orthopedic Group, Virginia Beach

"What a great effort in capturing the very best of why men long for the days of battle ... whether with a fishing rod, on the pitch, or just the everyday fight it takes to survive. A super reference for all that is wise."
>—Col. Tom Trumps (Ret.), Commandant
>Virginia Military Institute

The Book of Testosterone
by Mike Herron

© Copyright 2013 by Mike Herron

ISBN 9781938467585

All rights reserved. No part of this publication may be reproduced, stored in a retrieval system, or transmitted in any form or by any means – electronic, mechanical, photocopy, recording, or any other – without the prior written permission of the author.

Quotes and anecdotes are attributed to the authors wherever possible. The rest are either from the author's memory or belong to unknown men from the past.

Published by
köehlerbooks™
an imprint of Morgan James Publishing

5 Penn Plaza, 23rd floor
c/o Morgan James Publishing
New York, NY 10001
212-574-7939
www.koehlerbooks.com

Publisher
John Köehler

Executive Editor
Joe Coccaro

Habitat for Humanity
Peninsula and Greater Williamsburg
Building Partner

In an effort to support local communities, raise awareness and funds, Morgan James Publishing donates a percentage of all book sales for the life of each book to Habitat for Humanity Peninsula and Greater Williamsburg.
Get involved today, visit www.MorganJamesBuilds.com

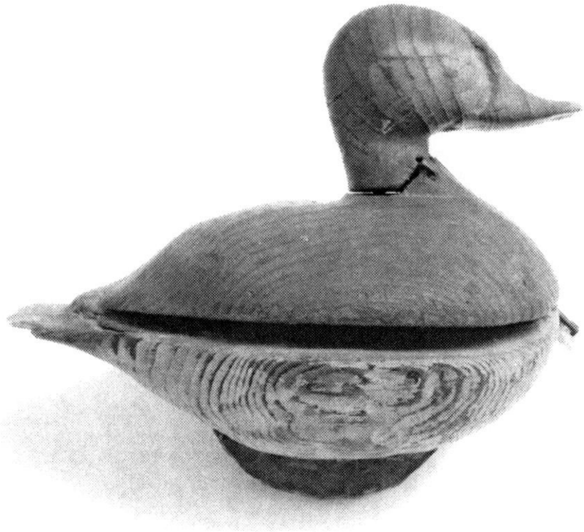

NOW
5 for 10¢
VIRGINIA
CHEROOTS
P. WHITLOCK
P. LORILLARD COMPANY
4 FOR 10 CENTS.

The Book of
Testosterone

Stuff Men Say

Mike Herron

NEW YORK
VIRGINIA

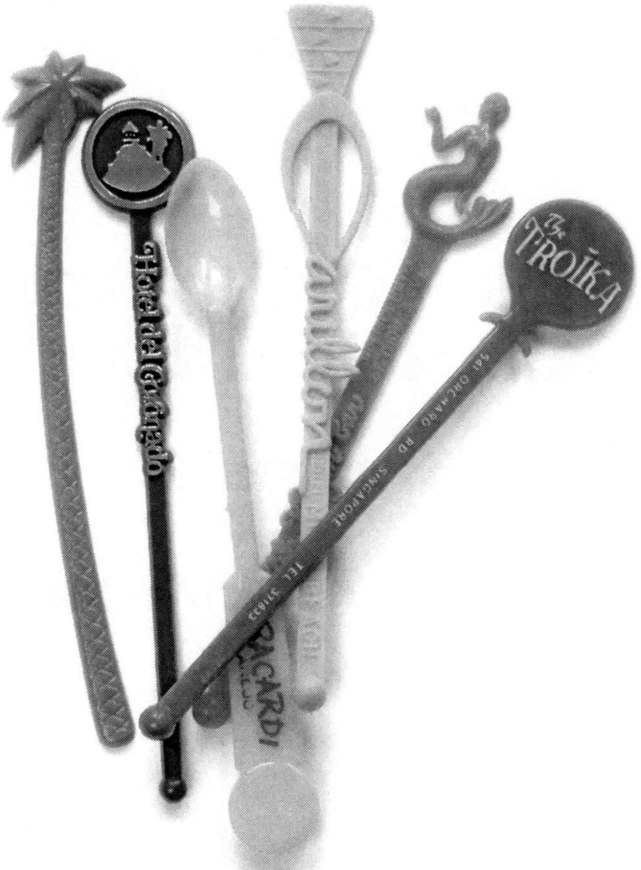
Hotel del Coronado
The TROIKA
BACARDI

This book is dedicated to the love of my life,

my wife, Elyse,

who enables me to live a full and meaningful life

while adding to my joy and happiness each day.

Oh, what a lucky man I am.

Contents

Mud and Blood and Beer

Attitude 8
Strength and Toughness 15
Respect 20
Drive and Effort 25
Humility 32
Communication 36

I'll Swig to That

Drinking 40
Hunting 44
Fishing 51
Fighting 58
Weapons 62
Wheels 68
Boating 72
Camping 75
Cooking 79
Women 83
Style 90

Shenanigans

Fun and Games 96
Competition and Sports 101
Animals and Nature 110
Living and Loving 115
People 120
Exercise and Health 126
Work and Labor 130

Gentlemen and Hacks

Religion and The Arts 136
Politics and Government 139
Business 144
The Military 152

Being Awake When it Matters

Intelligence and Learning 157
Survival 165
Leadership 170
Reality 175

FOREWORD

In the last couple of decades, over numerous smoky firepits, sipping various Scotch whiskeys and pints of home-brewed ales and beers—and usually with stogies lighted—but always in a crowd of his interesting friends, I've spent many an afternoon in Mike Herron's backyard cabana. An international sports game, typically rugby, plays incessantly on the background TV. Far beyond a "man cave," Mike's cabana overflows with more artifacts, collections, and exhibits than most small town museums. It is, in fact, a museum of testosterone. How fitting then that it was here, in this special place, that Mike first told me about his idea for this book.

I knew the book would be good, because everything Mike does tends to turn out good. I also expected it to be well written, because he is not only well-read himself, but as a publishing executive he's had more practice writing than most. More importantly, I expected it to be written well because Mike is quite simply an expert at living the rugged and adventurous lifestyle. As I leafed through the first pages of the final draft, I had to stop briefly to get in character. I grabbed a tall sipper of single malt Scotch, lighted a Cuban and started reading again, from the beginning. This is a book that you will want to read with a man's beverage and a fine cigar. You will agree that it is indeed well written and written well.

This book is influenced by Mike's late father, a combat Marine and Cold War CIA operative. It is also influenced by his son, a recent VMI graduate who is presently in the Marine Corps infantry. In fact, there are many such influences—an abridged list of whom is provided in the end.

I finished the book before I finished my cigar, which gave me time to realize what my friendship with Mike Herron has taught me. First, man stuff is hard work. You are going to sweat, a lot. Muscles aren't there for tanning—they're for exertion. Second, being a man isn't just fun, it's fun as hell. There's loads of laughter to go with all that work. And, third, learning about manhood—and yourself—is best done in the company and fellowship of men.

This is a book that fathers will share with sons, sons with fathers, brothers with brothers, and mates with mates. Women will also want to share it with the men in their lives. They may not understand, or agree with, all of the author's subtle lessons.

But their men will.

John Owens
Former Marine and Navy Fighter Pilot (Ret.)
CEO of Prevailance, Inc.

Mud and Blood and Beer

I like knocking heads in a rugby tournament, sitting up a tree in a deer stand waiting for a full-antlered buck to show itself, rambling through a farm field on an ATV at full throttle, and hooking a large tuna in the Gulf Stream. I like talking with my buddies about good-looking women and drinking from a keg on tap at the bar behind my house. I like hosing the mud caked on the bottom of my pick-up and a close shave after a week in the woods. I enjoy being home with my two eighty-pound-plus dogs, listening to my parrot talk to me every morning, and having a trained house rabbit that wakes me up each morning. And, best of all, my wife lets me be me—and she's a fox.

Do I really care if others judge me as a redneck, or macho, or a middle-aged Peter Pan, or weird, or extravagant, or even a Neanderthal? Hell no! And if you're a man, a real man, neither should you.

I enjoy myself the way I do because I have had great role models, men who have shown me the way to live a full life while simultaneously teaching me about being a man. They have encouraged me to nurture worthwhile friendships with other like-minded men.

I was given a head start because of the herd of men who

have been my tutors. It started with my grandfather, who was a famous sea captain and adventurer. The legacy was perpetuated by my father, who was a decorated combat Marine and field agent in the Central Intelligence Agency. These two men freely shared their passion for camaraderie and learning while exposing me to the value of physical activity and the outdoors throughout my childhood. They taught me right from wrong, without ambiguity, and engrained in me a love for others, God and country. They taught me discernment and critical thinking, and they gently carved in my heart the value of having fun.

My dad and grandad were both accomplished men, yet they placed more worth on a man's character than on his trophies or money. They understood that boys become gentlemen through osmosis, by being around chaps who have "been there and done that." Consequently, I found myself enjoying the company of an incredible cast of characters throughout my life, mainly through fishing, hunting, and my ongoing enjoyment of athletics and the outdoors.

Not all men are this fortunate. Not all have had as many desirable role models. Worse, some men have been emasculated by the wrong type of role models—weak wimps. I can think of many mealy-mouthed, faux intellectuals who inhabit our society's bureaucracy, government, academia, and our media and entertainment industries. These pantywaists obfuscate male insight, encourage males to be in touch with their "feminine side." They want men to repress the urge to be men, to soften the edges of being male. They confuse the role of men and marginalize the importance and contribution of manhood.

To develop into well-rounded real men, guys need advice and coaching from alpha males. Men deserve the perspectives of rugged males, refined through experiences exclusive to their gender. Such men harbor tons of practical knowledge so important to a man, but not very easily gained. This knowledge comes from those moments of truth that build strong character and discipline. This is the learning which should guide a man's behavior and ultimately bring him happiness and fulfillment. This is the process that shapes a man into what he ought to be, what he needs to be, what he was born to be.

Without the right mentoring, men will miss out on many concepts and critical information vital to our gender. Without the wisdom of alpha males, young men may end up with only the bitter end of the rope and sadly become less male and less happy.

Well, I am here to help fix that. I am here to help men attain manhood and to help women better understand men and encourage manhood.

The Book of Testosterone is a user manual that starts with the simple idea that the words testosterone and men are synonymous. We use testosterone as a literary device—not a scientific term. We're not here to discuss testicular hormone secretion or to encourage the use of steroids to goose athletic performance. Rather, we see testosterone as a symbol of traits the hormone provokes in men: strength and courage. Women can be strong and brave too. But just like the hormone itself, testosterone is primarily the domain of men.

When testosterone is embraced it can transform the host. It makes men tough, hard-working, and muscular, and honest. Real men, testosterone-driven men, do what is right, at all times—not only when it's convenient. They aren't lazy. They love the outdoors. They seek excitement—better yet, exhilaration.

They prefer speed over sloth, fight before flight, meat and potatoes. Real men make things happen, and their testosterone only thrives when their heart beats strong. Testosterone is the ingredient that enables male perspective and helps him relate to the real-man world around him.

Theodore Roosevelt summed it up perfectly:

> *It is not the critic who counts; not the man who points out how the strong man stumbles, or where the doer of deeds could have done them better. The credit belongs to the man who is actually in the arena, whose face is marred by dust and sweat and blood; who strives valiantly; who errs, who comes short again and again, because there is no effort without error and shortcoming; but who does actually strive to do the deeds; who knows great enthusiasms, the great devotions; who spends himself in a worthy cause; who at the best knows in the end the triumph of high achievement, and who at the worst, if he fails, at least fails while daring greatly, so that his place shall never be with those cold and timid souls who neither know victory nor defeat.*

Damn right! We don't need one more man missing the training—or being feminized—just to make the world a nice place. The world isn't a nice place. It can be difficult and complicated, and what it needs more than ever are real, full-blooded, able-bodied, well-developed men.

After I lost my father and then one friend after another,

I started to hear their words over and over. I realized their teachings were still with me and the profound effect of their opinions and advice. Their words have real and lasting value, so I share them here.

The Book of Testosterone is an array of euphemisms, clichés, observations, quotes, and advice. Some are meant to be humorous, but all have a message or noteworthy point. This book will inspire the ongoing process of becoming a man of substance. Its timeless knowledge is profoundly useful, having the value of shaping behavior, sharpening opinions, and adjusting attitudes.

Man-building isn't a dandified process, so this book isn't the answer; it's just a great start. Your journey to stir the testosterone within you will take hard work, self-awareness, and attention to detail. It will take a lot of sweat and time. Hopefully, this whimsical guide will help you become the man you were made to be.

The Book of Testosterone contains a great deal of sage wisdom, in the form of maxims, proverbs, idioms, anecdotes and common clichés, whose origination may be debated.

As a young teenager, when Belgium was invaded by the Germans during WWI, my grandfather was thrown into prison on suspicion of shooting an occupying soldier. When Antwerp was bombed, his section of the prison was blown to bits. This piece of shrapnel had lodged in his bedpost, and as he fled the wreckage, he grabbed it for a souvenir. He gave it to me shortly before his death and told me it was his reminder of how blessed he was. He told me how blessed I was to live in a free country. It has always been my most valued possession.

> I never lost faith in the end of the story. I never doubted not only that I would get out, but also that I would prevail in the end and turn the experience into the defining event of my life, which, in retrospect, I would not trade.
>
> JIM STOCKDALE, POW

To err is human, to forgive divine;
neither of which is Marine Corps policy.

U̲nknown

This is my dad's Marine Corps ashtray. My father joined the Marine Corps at seventeen. He used to joke that he thought "semper fidelis" meant seventy-five dollars. He was in the Pearl Harbor Navy Yard on December 7, 1941, "when the planes came over" and was with the First Marine Division when they hit the beaches at Okinawa and Guadalcanal. The Marines taught my father a lot about life and death, and as tough as it could be sometimes, I was blessed to be raised by one.

Attitude

Testosterone is, above all, an attitude—one that will bolster the outcome of just about everything you do. When you start with enthusiasm, confidence, or willingness and desire—versus their alternatives—better results are inevitable. With a testosterone attitude, successes become more common and significant. A little attitude adjustment helps to overcome inadequacies and hurdles.

A positive attitude multiplies the quality of everything—your effort, determination, intensity, calmness, insight, focus, input, output, spirit, and sanity. Testosterone influences your level of success. Better yet, testosterone can make all the difference you'll need.

Lance Van de Castle played four years of college football and twice won the Scottish Highland Games in Virginia. In his prime, he was one of the top rugby players in the United States. Lance had the most positive attitude of anyone I have ever met. He loved life, which our mutual friend Alan Larivee pointed out, he strolled through like Hercules. He was a dear friend to many. After he died in an automobile accident in 2007, more than seven hundred people attended his funeral in the small mountain community of Madison, Virginia. This was clear testimony to what a great man he was, and obviously to the power of a great disposition.

Here I am with my brother and some college friends, sitting on his barn roof, taking in the scenery. Sometimes the best attitude is to not have a care in the world.

It is far better to be a participant than a spectator.

"A man can be destroyed but not defeated."
Ernest Hemingway

Try to give folks what they want.

A handshake doesn't count unless it's firm.

Talk is cheap. Actions speak louder than words.

I will never quit .... I will not fail.
U.S. Navy SEAL Pledge

When you bury the hatchet,
make sure it isn't in someone's head.

How much more grievous are the consequences
of anger than the causes of it.
Marcus Aurelius

When someone invades your personal space, don't step back—
instead, step forward.

For a short time, I worked in the shipyard on the hose gang. My favorite job was hooking up saltwater fire hoses whenever ships were moved. I think that is how a plumber's wrench got nicknamed a monkey wrench. It takes a monkey to wrestle a fire hose.

> "It's my rule never to lose me temper,
> till it would be detrimental to keep it."
> SEAN O'CASEY

When you have the opportunity to take a nap, go for it.

We will either find a way, or make one.
HANNIBAL

Member John Day, of Medford, Oregon, and his King-size Kodiak
The skin measures 11' 8" wide, 10' 2" long and the skull is 12½" thick

My grandfather was active in the Explorers Club and was on the board of The Adventurers Club of New York, which put out the magazine above. This copy is signed by his good friend John Day. While the aim of these were to share incredible accomplishments, as you read them, you realize that it was the attitudes and spirit of these men, rather than their physical gifts, that produced their wondrous accomplishments.

Looking forwards is far more productive than looking backwards, yet living in the present is what matters.

———

Variety is the spice of life.
Don't go through life like a single food eater.

———

If all you have is a hammer, everything looks like a nail.
From Abraham Maslow

———

If you must face the music, dance to it.

Strength and Toughness

Even if testosterone sets you up for success, life brings difficulties and challenges. Health, work, money, family, and relationships in general, can all put you in a bind. Having enough testosterone to deal with these hurdles—and there is never enough—will noticeably improve your life. In a testosterone world, you're always resilient and resourceful.

I have a bar (man-hut) behind my house. I enjoy it often. No one at the bar tolerates complaints, so my good friend Roger Herring, who disallowed the words shoulda, coulda, and woulda from his vocabulary, made me this handwrit sign. It speaks volumes.

There is no such place as Easy Street.

No whining.

Pain is a fact of life; suffering is optional.

———

You can't have a testimony without a test.

———

If you don't have a few scars, something is wrong.

———

You've got to break a few eggs to make an omelet.

———

What does not destroy me makes me stronger.
FRIEDRICH NIETZSCHE

———

An appeaser is one who feeds a crocodile,
hoping it will eat him last.
SIR WINSTON CHURCHILL

I will never quit.

I persevere and thrive on adversity. My Nation expects me to be physically harder and mentally stronger than my enemies. If knocked down, I will get back up, every time. I will draw on every remaining ounce of strength to protect my teammates and to accomplish our mission.

I am never out of the fight.

A CREDO OF THE U.S. NAVY SEALS

If you can't cure it, just endure it.

Don't mess with old men;
they didn't get old by being stupid.

Life cuts both ways.
No need to overreact when things don't go your way.

The road is usually hard,
even without the bumps.

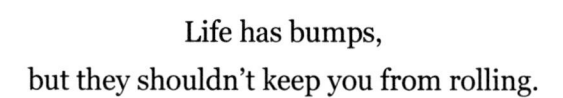

Life has bumps,
but they shouldn't keep you from rolling.

For he today that sheds his blood
with me, Shall be my brother ...
WILLIAM SHAKESPEARE

Life is a full contact sport.

My father was 100% Irish. This was his Shillelagh. He got it from "The Old Sod"— Ireland, where old guys carry these sticks. Born tough, as he got older and wiser, he became even tougher. Anyone who dared mess with my dad's testosterone was making a big mistake.

U.S. Navy binoculars

Respect

Men aren't born with the respect of others. Respect is hard-earned and easy to lose. We are born with instincts, but it's education and experience that determines how we live and how we're viewed by others. A man's testosterone helps him decide what deserves his attention, what are his priorities, and what's worthy of his indulgence.

This picture was first published in Rugby Magazine after the Cardinals Rugby Club won The Fort Lauderdale International 45+ Division. In it, from left to right are Steve Walters, John Carr, Danny Lonergan, and me; all former players with the Norfolk City Blues R.F.C., along with Lance Van de Castle and Terry Whelan of the Virginia Rugby Club.

After the Marine Corps, my father worked as a Special Investigator in Manhattan, for which he was awarded the New York State Conspicuous Service Cross. He was recruited by the Central Intelligence Agency, where he spent thirty-seven years in operational assignments. Here he is in Kandahar, Afghanistan. He traveled extensively throughout the world, and became fluent in German and conversational in Chinese. He graduated from American University. My father remained a good and humble man up until his death. He never missed an opportunity to give a bit of himself to all who passed his way. He always had my utmost respect.

Respect yourself regardless of your difficulties.

Every so often the dog has to battle the bear
just so he can call himself a dog again.
WILLIAM FAULKNER

When you cheat, everything is diminished.

Don't make people the butt of your jokes.

Don't let familiarity exceed the bounds of respect.

Don't look a gift horse in the mouth.

If it's worth showing up for, it's worth being on time.

Civility costs nothing,
but not everyone deserves yours.

Tip waitresses handsomely and don't forget
to buy a few rounds. Being cheap is being a creep.

Never enjoy the misfortunes of others.

Respect the police, and when dealing with them,
the only correct responses are "yes sir" and "no sir."

Quietly enjoy the luxury of turning down unwanted invitations.

Keep traditions alive. You'll be glad you did.

Drive and Effort

Testosterone determines our level of drive, effort, and commitment. It differentiates us from wimps. There is a wide gap between being involved and being committed. And when things don't go as planned, testosterone finds a way to make things happen.

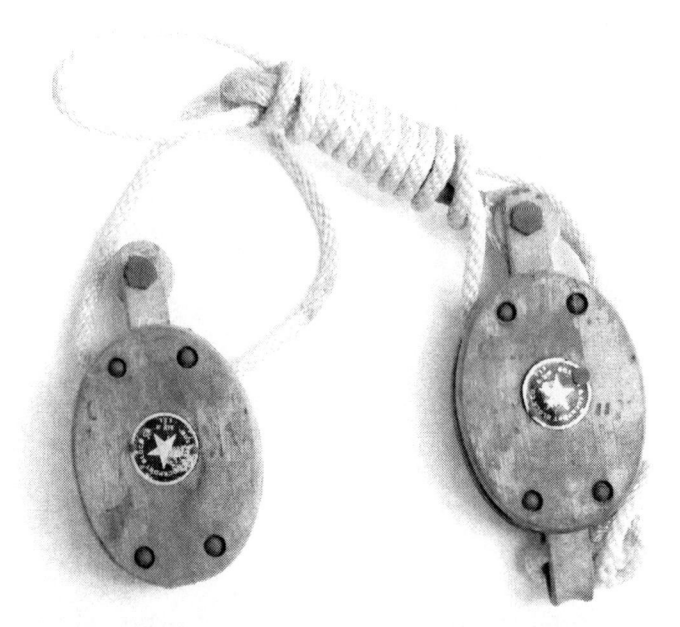

The Block and Tackle is just one of many tools to use when things don't go your way. Brawn isn't always the answer; using your head is always the preferred option.

A killer-instinct is God-given.

To whom much is given, much is expected.

Stand up, and give it to him!
HERMAN MELVILLE

You own your own motivation.

Now is the best mindset.

A kick in the ass moves one forward.

Go ahead, make my day.
Clint Eastwood in *Dirty Harry*
(H. Fink, R. Fink & Dean Riesner)

Work hard. Every other option is less productive.

Doubts corrupt your spirit, so don't give them any mind.

When you know you're right, don't compromise.

This is a 2 foot X 10 inch log a beaver carved down on both ends, along with the upper jaw of a beaver, showing the incisors. The eager beaver is one of God's most industrious creatures and can provide us all inspiration. With the right goal, drive and determination become second nature.

>A full belly is not always a good thing.
>Sometimes it pays to be hungry.

You've got to kick the devil in the ass every day.

Full-tilt boogie is an excellent speed.

Procrastination doesn't save a minute of time.

It's alright to have lots to do, just don't overdo it.

Be careful for what you wish for, as you just may get it.

... a life of ease is not for any man, nor for any god.
THOMAS CARLYLE

If it's worth doing a job, it's worth doing it well—particularly the first time.

Many assume practice is work. Try shooting a box of skeet. Practice couldn't be more fun.

The early bird really does get the worm.

You mustn't ask too much of human endurance ...
Fyodor Dostoyevsky

Preparation and practice produce improved results. Practice is what leads to skills.

Entertainers almost always have more nerve than talent.

Virtue, like art, constantly deals with what is hard to do,
and the harder the task the better the success.
A%%%%ristotle

Nothing is a right which has to be produced by human toil.

It's hard to hit a moving target, so keep moving.

Any fool can make a rule, and any fool will mind it.
H%%%%enry D%%%%avid T%%%%horeau

Some rules really are made to be broken.

Stick to your resolve.

Humility

I once had the opportunity to spend the better part of a day with Jesse Owens, the great Olympic athlete. At lunch that day, he spoke and answered questions graciously. He listened with intense focus to the others around him, almost apathetic to his own importance. I had been taught that humility was the greatest virtue, and on that day, I sat humbled in its company.

If you are going to master something,
master self-control.

Keep your conscience alive.
You have to live with yourself.

Captain Lawrence J. Hasse was my maternal grandfather. After surviving the occupation of Belgium in World War I, he became a decorated U.S. Navy captain in World War II. Among his many leadership positions, he was president of the Master Mariners of America. A worldwide seaman all his life, when he retired he owned the Larcon Marina in St. Petersburg, Florida, building and refurbishing sport fishing boats. In his day he was likely the best angler in all of Florida. As a big guy, also heavily tattooed, he could be quite intimidating. Yet he always remained humble. In 1982 he was buried in Arlington National Cemetery with full military honors.

Selfishness is the opposite of love.

Egos are for assholes.

Judge not, that ye be not judged.
THE BIBLE

Don't make promises ... they can be hard to keep.

One thing on which all
craftsmen agree—everyone
who has a vice needs a vise.

    And often times excusing of a fault
    doth make the fault the worse by the excuse.
          WILLIAM SHAKESPEARE

Take the high road, and enjoy a much better view.

You never make yourself look good
by making others look bad.

Self-made men patronize their creator.

No living man belongs on a pedestal.

Don't be a show-off. Never be too proud to turn back.
There are old pilots and bold pilots, but no old, bold pilots.
E. Hamilton Lee

Whenever you're brilliant,
you're going to struggle with humility.

Know your limitations.

My father traveled along parts of the Amazon. This is one of the arrows he brought back with a long bow and quiver. When you realize that you're not as well armed as the natives, you learn humility real quick.

Communication

Testosterone is a straight shooter, and that means a straight communicator as well. Making things happen, which is testosterone's bias, takes verbal talent. Sharing your testosterone with others will provide you endless lifelong entertainment.

Listen more than you talk.
That's why you have one mouth and two ears.

Whatever is said after the words but or however is what one really thinks. Everything said before them is just posturing.

Make sure most of your stories are true.

The most appropriate reply to someone's drama:
"You must be confusing me with
someone who cares."

Good writing is rewriting.

The most fun word in the English
language to say is "Checkmate."

The New Shorter Oxford Dictionary
may not be short, but it is valuable.

You can't bullshit a bullshitter.

The simplest explanation is usually the best.

Leave gossip to women.

Too much exaggeration is lying.

Too much honesty
can ruin a marriage.

A half-truth is also
known as a lie.

A man's word goes a long way,
as long as he keeps it.

This is an Indian Talking Stick. It comes in handy at my bar, because it is customary that whoever is holding the stick is free to talk, while others must remain silent. It is such a great idea, we regularly employ the same tactic at our hunt camp, using "the feather" instead.

I'll Swig to That

Even if shot glasses are not designed to make you tell the truth, sometimes they're useful in that regard.

Drinking

Testosterone may give one the impression that it's a professional drinker, but it prefers to consider itself an amateur. It understands alcohol is called firewater for a reason. It can ruin your health, your marriage, your job, your life. Even so, testosterone realizes a libation can be a stress reliever and great way to enjoy oneself, but it also understands who is supposed to be in control.

Only drink when you're thirsty or when you're not.

An Irishman is never drunk as long as he can hold on to one
blade of grass and not fall off the face of the earth.
At least that's what the Irish think.

Beer is proof that God loves us
and wants us to be happy.
ATTRIBUTED TO BENJAMIN FRANKLIN

An open bar beats a buffet every time.

A Guinness a day keeps the doctor away,
unless he's a friend.

Scotch with a splash is a better choice than
Scotch on the rocks,
because that way you can drink more Scotch.

Through osmosis, and some well-intentioned elbow-bending, my father imprinted an appreciation for Tullamore Dew Irish Whiskey on me. Although he could extol its virtues with panache, I've grown to enjoy those memories even more than the drink itself, which is worth the swig.

When you get drunk,
it's not the bartender's fault.

Bushmills is the oldest Irish Whiskey,
and Jameson is very fine; however,
Tullamore Dew is my favorite.

———

Buy a round at the pub occasionally.
It's a great way to make friends.

———

Memorize at least one good toast.

Gosling's Rum from Bermuda is very, very fine.
Green Island Rum from Mauritius is very, very rare.

Drink to me.
PABLO PICASSO ON HIS DEATH BED

It's wonderful that Jack Daniel's whiskey is in a square bottle,
because it can't roll away from you.

One benefit of Glenfiddich Scotch's triangular bottle
is you can hide it in the corner of the cupboard.

When I read about the evils of drinking,
I gave up reading.
PAUL HORNUNG

In their own right,
stouts, porters, lagers and ales
are all excellent.

Hunting

Hunting is one of the most testosterone-injected experiences a man can enjoy. Hunting is complex while relaxing, and it is more sport than work. It can be dangerous, but it has the ability to make one better appreciate and cherish nature. Testosterone defines a man's place in the food chain, unveiling his primeval nature and exposing his limitations. While hunting can be solitary, at the same time it can build bonds that will last a lifetime. Providing food for testosterone and life for the soul, it is an extremely worthwhile endeavor.

Tony Bird has been a hunting partner of mine for more than twenty years. He took this elk in Colorado with bow and arrow. A former Navy SEAL, Tony continues to challenge and impress anyone who tries to keep up with him in the woods. I'm glad he's on my side.

<blockquote>The most essential component to success in hunting is local knowledge.</blockquote>

<blockquote>Know your target, and beyond.</blockquote>

The picture above is my hunting buddy Maurice Childers with a Safari Club World Record caribou taken with a black powder rifle in Northern Labrador. Maurice is one of those hunters who works as hard in the off-season as he does during it and it consistently shows in his productivity harvesting game.

If you kill it, you should eat it.

Here is Mick White, one of my rugby teammates, with a fifteen-point buck he took in Franklin, Virginia. Particularly with close friends, success is shared and everyone is proud of difficult accomplishments.

Never run from an animal.
Face the danger, and back up slowly if you must.

To improve game habitat, plant milo and clover.

The definition of success—four bucks taken on one weekend. From left to right: Mike Herron, Roger Herring, Jay Herring, Tony Bird.

Hunt with the wind in your face and the sun at your back.

When you have your prey in your crosshairs,
relax, it's all over.

Shoot as many times as you need.
There is no such thing as too dead.

Washing clothes in ammonia removes scent.

―――

When hunting big game,
move your eyes more than your head.

―――

Join Ducks Unlimited.

―――

Own a good pair of high mud boots.

Pulling in Atlantic stripers (rockfish) two at a time on Top Notch, just off Virginia Beach, a sportsman's paradise.

Unfortunately, it's easy to waste fish when cleaning them for food. Here, a creative fisherman addressed that by turning a marlin's bill into a fillet knife.

Fishing

Fishing is a testosterone paradox of excitement and serenity. My father and grandfather instilled in me a love for angling, and it has lasted throughout my life.

My grandfather had two careers on the sea—one as a merchant seaman and another one as an officer in the U.S. Navy. Those two bank accounts provided him enough to buy some commercial waterfront and build a marina. As owner and operator of the Larcon Marina in St. Petersburg, Florida, he began to refurbish sport-fishing boats and fish whenever he could.

At a very early age, he imprinted on my brother and me the wonders of fishing. I learned to fish often and to fish late. Throwing bait or a lure from a dock, boat, or shore, and using your wits to land a fish are hard to beat. In Florida, we'd fish off the piers, and sometimes off the beach, but when we were really lucky, we'd fish on one of my grandfather's boats out in the Gulf of Mexico. My grandfather loved to catch mackerel, or kingfish, their bigger brothers, which were prolific in those waters. We would troll for them, while he would drive his boat. Both are oily fish, so they smoke well. My grandfather had built a couple of smokers, and they remained active.

With all the wonderful-tasting fish in the oceans, smoked mackerel remains my favorite fish to eat.

My father saw how much I enjoyed fishing, and so he too began to nurture it. He would regularly take me to rural lakes and rivers in Virginia, and drop me off for the day. When I was young, I'd get so excited when I got a bite that I'd lose a lot of fish. I quickly learned how to "let the fish take the hook," and since those early successes, I have never stopped fishing.

As I got older, my father would listen attentively to my blow-by-blow reenactments of fishing experiences in the Pacific, the Caribbean, Mexico, out West, or off Virginia Beach, where I live. But those trips never matched up to the experiences we shared together. My strongest memory of fishing with my father was when he had scouted out a famous fishing ground near Aripeka, east of Tampa. The fishing camp he had located was where Jack Dempsey, Babe Ruth, and other sportsmen of his youth would go to fish and play cards. The place held some mystique with

Here is Tony See with a steelhead trout caught on the Salmon River in Idaho.

my dad. When we first got there, we rented a small boat with an outboard motor and loaded it with cold beer and fishing tackle. As we began to make our way, motoring from fresh water to salt water, through beautiful low-slung oak trees strung with Spanish moss, fish were literally jumping all around us. Unfortunately, these were mullet, vegetarians who wanted nothing to do with our live minnows. No problem; we had plenty of cold beer. Nevertheless, it is frustrating when you're casting feverishly, while fish jump all around you, and you don't get a single bite. We pretended it didn't matter. It was a beautiful afternoon, yet we had run out of beer without having a single fish in the well. We cranked up the outboard and headed back to the dock. Once we arrived, it was up to me to clean the boat, as Dad was paying the tab. When I threw our last minnows overboard, I noticed an unmistakable ripple in the water, right near the dock. Fortunately, one of the minnows had landed on the deck instead of in the water. I hooked that last minnow, still flopping with life, and dropped it right off the dock instead of casting it. Sure enough, almost on demand, a huge largemouth bass rose to the surface. As his jaws opened, its size was breathtaking. It was the "Big One" that all fishermen dream about. As I saw its jaws surround the bait, I let the fish take the hook almost to the bottom before I jerked my rod. When I reeled him in, and then held him high in the air, he was hard to hold up. My dad, who was coming out of the bait shack, proclaimed it the biggest freshwater fish he'd ever seen. After some angst, we decided the fish was too big to keep. I slipped him back in the water, holding him steady until the water brought energy back into his life, and then gingerly let him go. We just stood there taking in the moment.

Here is a barracuda caught and released just off "Hole in the Wall" near Freeport in the Bahamas.

Big fish will take a big hook, but smaller fish can't.
If you want to eat, don't overdo your bait.

Fishing right is fishing at night.

Don't hesitate to kill water snakes.
They eat millions of fish eggs.

Don't keep a fish with a bloated belly; it likely contains a thousand fish yet to be born. Take a photograph instead.

In freshwater fishing,
the difficult places to fish are likely where there are fish.

Let the fish take the hook before you pull the rod.

Chumming isn't cheating.

One of the greatest benefits of fishing is it's the best way to spend time with the people you care about. I took this picture of my good friend Dennis Ellmer, on one of his boats, pulling in a beautiful (and delicious!) spadefish.

> The most significant ingredient to success in fishing is local knowledge.

> Old fish like new flies.

> Fish like shade too,
> so cast to the edge of weeds or lily pads.

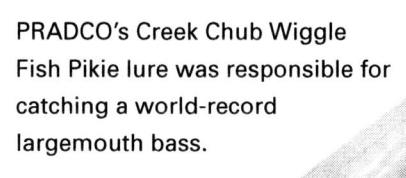

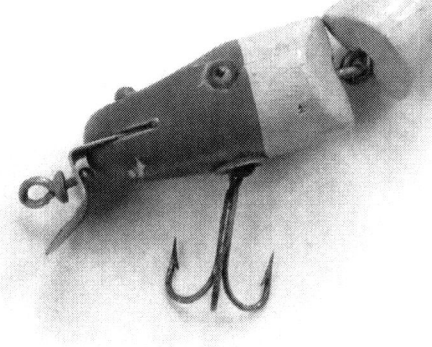

PRADCO's Creek Chub Wiggle Fish Pikie lure was responsible for catching a world-record largemouth bass.

The best freshwater bass lure is the
Fred Arbogast Hula Popper.

Use the Solunar Tables.
Fish bite at the change of the tides.

When fishing with spinners, troll deep and slow.

It is a wonderful thing when you throw a fish back.

Fighting

"WHAT did you say?"

Yep, that's how it usually starts—a testosterone comment, or a misplaced answer. Sometimes testosterone can't help but be in the wrong place at the wrong time, which may improve the odds for some fisticuffs. I've been in an unfair share of fights. Thank God and my other father I had a little testosterone instruction. My father boxed when he was in high school, and so we had a pair of boxing gloves in our house when I was growing up. Whenever I had a major disagreement with my older brother, we'd end up out in the backyard, with me receiving some worthwhile instruction from those boxing gloves. It kind of put the bickering to a minimum. In most every way, my dad was brilliant.

Be very aware of the sucker punch.

The bigger they are, the harder they fall.

"He can run, but he can't hide."
JOE LOUIS REGARDING BILLY CONN

A good pair of boxing gloves not only protects your hands, they build upper-arm strength.

Fights usually bring an audience.

If the loser goes to the hospital, the winner may go to jail.

In fighting, when confronted by a much larger man,
it is advisable to put him on the ground as quickly as you can.
There, his size becomes much less of a problem.

Let the other guy start the fight.
You'll stand a better chance of finishing it.

My business is hurting people.
Sugar Ray Robinson

Punch with more than just your weight.
Punch with your heart.

Fight for a cause.

The jab is the most important punch in boxing.
The most important skill to master is
not telegraphing all the others.

Rules no longer apply.
THE MARQUIS OF QUEENSBERRY

The only undefeated heavyweight champion was
Rocky Marciano at 49-0. He defended his title six times.
He had 43 wins by knockouts, including KOs of
Jersey Joe Walcott and Joe Louis.

When you tell someone you're going to kick their ass,
you usually end up losing the fight.

I just forgot to duck.
JACK DEMPSEY AFTER LOSING THE HEAVYWEIGHT TITLE
TO GENE TUNNEY

Weapons

Weapons have a function, and therefore testosterone consigns them their proper place. They are for protection, utility, and sporting fun. Understand their dangers while knowing and enjoying their power.

Don't bring a knife to a gunfight.

HAVE GUN WILL TRAVEL
WIRE PALADIN
SAN FRANCISCO

Like most men, I was first introduced to guns and weapons by watching Westerns as a young boy. This is an original card used in the filming of the television series *Paladin*, which was given to me by a friend of my father's when I was ten years old.

Ready ... Aim ... Fire.
That order is very important.

A revolver will never have a hair-trigger, but a pistol may.

Always buy the best ammunition you can afford.

Clean your guns soon after use. Rust never sleeps.

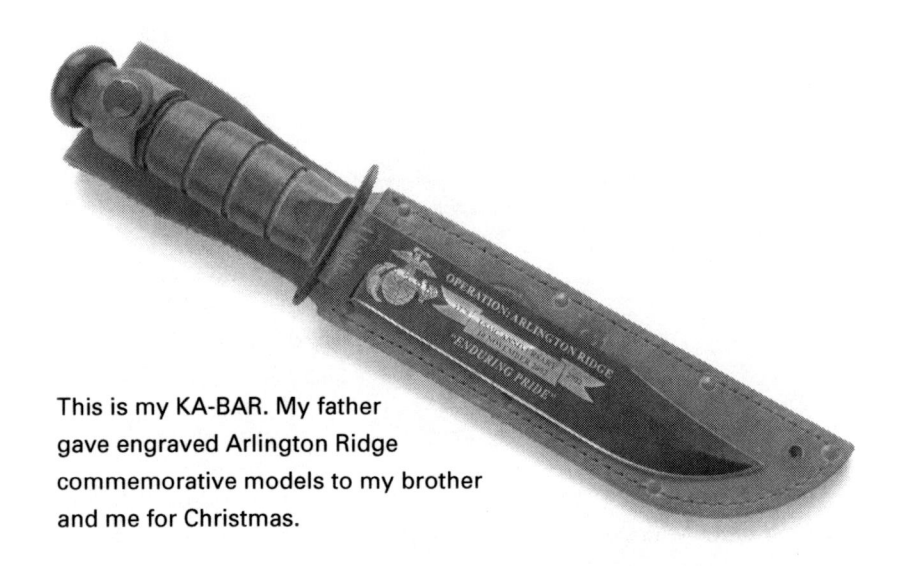

This is my KA-BAR. My father gave engraved Arlington Ridge commemorative models to my brother and me for Christmas.

If you want a real knife, get yourself a KA-BAR.

Correctly judging distance will help
you become a good shot.

Happiness is a warm gun.
THE BEATLES

It is better to have a poor weapon
in the hands of a good shooter
than a good weapon in the hands of a poor shooter.

It takes at least a hundred practice shots
to hit one bull's-eye.

———

When a knife has a blood groove,
the knife is for something other than spreading butter.

———

Muzzle control is controlling barrel direction.
When holding a weapon it must never cease.

———

There isn't a day of the week you shouldn't
carry a pocket knife.

———

The safest way to carry a gun is
on the shoulder with the muzzle up.

This is the Super Magnum Remington 870 Express 12-gauge, one of three I own. It is the best-selling shotgun of all time for a reason.

With a gun there is no second chance.

There really are silver bullets.

The right amount of ammunition is too much ammunition.

When in doubt, empty the magazine.

My shotgun-shell belt used for duck hunting. You don't ever want to run out of ammunition.

Treat all guns, at all times, as if they are loaded.

You don't pull a trigger, you squeeze it.

You must sight-in your own rifle.

A gun safe is a valuable investment.

Guns don't kill people, people kill people.

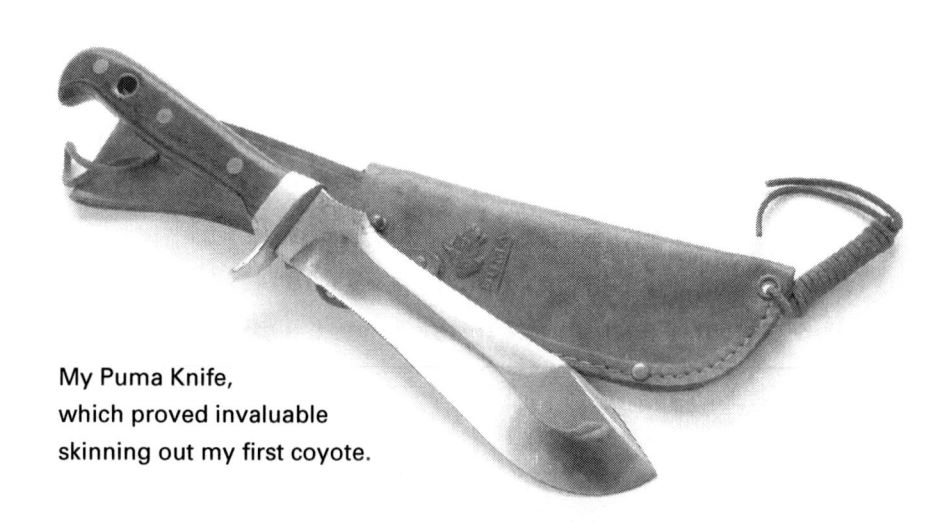

My Puma Knife,
which proved invaluable
skinning out my first coyote.

ATVs provide a lot of entertainment and we've got quite a few at our hunting camp. Here's Gene Jernigan on a three-wheeler, one of the more challenging ones to ride.

Wheels

Testosterone is drawn to things that have motors in them—from cars to trucks, tractors to motorcycles, trains to airplanes, it doesn't matter. It's their mechanical nature that intrigues, and testosterone plays a role in keeping them running. The fact that they move at varying speeds, and have their own style, gives testosterone unique comfort and allows it to be in control. No wonder men of testosterone invest so much in them.

You don't always have to start in first gear,
second gear often works just fine.

Only a moron runs out of gas.

Change your vehicle's oil every 5,000 miles.

Change your vehicle's hoses and belts
as often as you change its tires.

Every vehicle's trunk should contain jumper cables
and a can of Fix-A-Flat.

It always pays to do a dry run on changing tires.

Here I am when I was a beach lifeguard, with my second racing bike, a KZ-900. At the time it was the fastest stock motorcycle in the world. It didn't stay stock for very long; I upgraded it with headers, new carburetors, and better tires. The dune-buggy behind me was custom-built by one of my good friends, Bob House, who took this picture. Life is a journey, and if you follow the right advice, it is a blast.

Everyone who buys a motorcycle
that isn't a Harley-Davidson
wishes they'd bought a Harley-Davidson.

Whenever possible, use cruise control.

Forgo a camper;
buy a Chevrolet Suburban instead.

The fewer the exhaust pipes on a motorcycle,
the better the horsepower.

There must be an obvious reason the Ford F-150
is the best-selling truck of all time.

Treat your vehicle windshield with Rain-X.
Visibility is a great thing.

Since white tends to reflect light and is easier to see,
it makes a great vehicle color.

Here's Will Crell (on right) with his first mate out on the Chesapeake Bay sailing in one of his Drascombe Luggers. This is relaxation at its pinnacle.

Boating

My grandfather bought my brother and me a sailboat as soon as we learned how to swim. I've been jumping in boats ever since. My close friend Roger Herring, when we were roommates, owned nineteen boats. There is something about boats that lures testosterone. If it isn't fishing, it's getting underway, whether by engine power or under sail. The journey is usually an adventure. The destinations and a safe return make it all worthwhile.

A trailing wind fills all sails.

In navigation, remember the buoys are set up
"Red - Right - Return."

Never dive unless you know the depth,
and what's on the bottom is always
closer than it looks.

Before setting or resetting your anchor,
make sure it's first secured to the boat.

Keep your boat shipshape and in Bristol fashion.
If the weather picks up,
you don't want a victory at sea.

Keep your nose to the wind
and your eyes on the horizon.

This is the fifty-four-foot sport fishing boat Top Notch, the third of four boats of that name, built by my friend Russ Kostinas and his brother Gene. It is chartered out of Rudee Inlet in Virginia Beach. I have fished with Russ for over twenty years filling cooler after cooler with fish from the Atlantic. The Top Notch is top notch.

The best boat is a friend's boat.

The only rope on a boat is the one tied to the anchor;
all others are lines.

The square knot is the most often used, but
the bowline knot is the most important one to master.

Your two happiest days of boat ownership will be
the day you buy it and the day you sell it.

A few campfire pals, like Howard Tew and Gene Jernigan, make standing around in the freezing cold feel like Jamaica. Having the proper clothing shouldn't be underestimated.

Camping

When you spend time in the outdoors, falling in love with Mother Nature is predictable. When in the outdoors for an extended period, "camp" becomes "home." As such, you need to set it up for fun, comfort, and safety. In the world of testosterone, it pays to do it up right.

Don't miss our national parks,
particularly Yellowstone.

Leaves of three; let them be.

Mink oil is the best protectant for leather.

Oxygen is the most important ingredient for a fire.

Sub-zero conditions call for long-sleeve mittens.

Pack wisely by traveling light. Limit your backpack to forty pounds, even if you think you're a mule.

The map is not the territory.
ALFRED KORZYBSKI

It's not a great camping trip without some fun and games. Here's some extracurricular activity at our hunt camp (certain activities require private property). Fireworks are always more exciting at night.

Don't pee in the well.
You may need to drink from it later.

Take care of your gear,
and your gear will take care of you.

Beef jerky should be in every backpack.

A pee bottle in a sleeping bag can come in real handy.

At times, toilet paper in a backpack
is more vital than a compass.

Red sky at night means camper's delight.
Red sky in morning means camper's warning.

When you pitch your tent, plan for rain runoff,
even when it doesn't look like rain.

Always pee on the downstream.

Lint is a great fire-starter.

Nature is a hanging judge.
Always be prepared for judgment day.

Cooking

Testosterone requires regular and ample feeding. Sometimes we need to take things into our own hands. When you want food done right, or as preferred, you may need to do it yourself. It shouldn't be lost on any of us that many of the world's great chefs are men and that cooking is an art, one with immediate dividends.

The keys to cooking are butter and salt.

Marinade whenever possible.

Arguably, the best cut of steak is the Porterhouse.

French and Italian food are all you'll ever need,
but if you have to live your life over,
live it over a Chinese restaurant.

Hotdogs aren't good for you, but they sure are good.

If you are picking up the tab,
you should be ordering the wine.

A real hot fire is the key to cooking a great steak.

If you desire superior rice, cook it with coconut milk.

The best cut of venison is the inside tenderloin,
better known as "The Preacher's Meat."

For simplicity and satisfaction, you can't beat a good BLT.

Cooking should be fun. Your approach is everything. Open up your mind, and maybe even some wine, and let your creative juices flow.

Nothing is sweeter than honey.

Restaurants that serve catfish usually have something going for them.

Sniffing the cork is a pretentious waste of time.
Taste the wine instead.

When deep frying fish, as soon as it floats, it's done.

To age venison properly, don't wrap it,
but rather expose it for ten days openly in the refrigerator.

You can't go wrong with peanut butter.

Never trust a skinny cook.

Just like in the workshop, there is a tool for most everything in the kitchen. These are my meat hammers, which are indispensable in tenderizing any less than perfect cuts of meat.

Women

Testosterone clearly expresses itself when in contact with the opposite sex (estrogen). Those expressions can obviously lead to fun and ecstasy, but they may also lead to pain and suffering. It all depends on the contrasts we choose. The best practice is consistency and care when indulging in women and their different ways.

> A man is only as young as the woman he feels.
> GROUCHO MARX

Marry late.

Jealousy gets you nowhere.

No friggin' in the riggin'.

Always remain discreet.

Your relationships should be monogamous ... mostly.

Always stand your ground; however, there is no shame in running from a woman.

Above all, women want someone to listen to them.

Some blondes are smarter than you.

The easiest way to get somewhere with a woman
is to ask her a lot of questions.

Sometimes the reason a divorce is expensive
is because it's worth it.

Premenstrual syndrome may bring out
the woman you really don't want to know.

Defend your Queen,
whether you're playing chess or not.

A woman with expensive tastes
should quickly become someone else's woman.

Candles do help set the mood.

If it's got breasts or disc brakes, it's got problems.

Never marry a woman for her mind or her body.
Marry her for her personality.

If a woman gets aggressive when drinking,
it's time to find another woman.

Instead of trying to find a woman's erogenous zone,
focus on her entire body.

It is never unadvisable to bring a woman flowers.

It's more than likely a woman
will end up looking like her mother.

Women love to dance.
If you don't, you're going to miss a huge opportunity.

Women who help their men pursue their interests end up more significant in the lives of those men. Here is my wife with me at a United States Rugby Football Foundation dinner in Aspen, lifting me up by facilitating my pastimes.

The way to a woman's heart is a good massage.

Particularly with women,
good things come to those who wait.

Women are not property.

It's alright to let a woman think she is in charge.

Some women can be like fishing lures;
they come with hooks.

Daughters (like my Meg) make fathers better men.

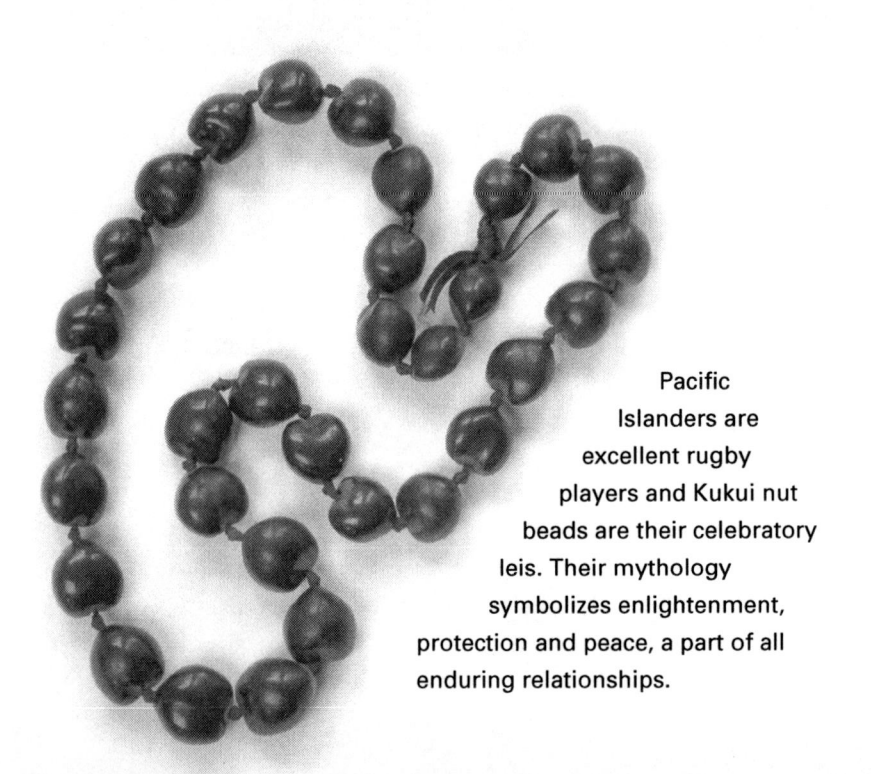

Pacific Islanders are excellent rugby players and Kukui nut beads are their celebratory leis. Their mythology symbolizes enlightenment, protection and peace, a part of all enduring relationships.

Unfortunately,
money makes a difference to some women.

———

When you first meet a woman, don't be bashful.
An interview isn't anytime to be humble.

———

With both women and cars, looks matter,
but it's what's under the hood that counts.

———

Women want men to be the dominant one during sex …
most of the time.

———

When a woman has no interest in fitness,
it's going to be easier to lose interest in her.

———

Never trust a woman's tears.
Fyodor Dostoyevsky

A Montblanc fountain pen qualifies as the world's best writing instrument.

Style

Every man has a certain style, whether contrived or not. It pays for a man to be aware of his. Style affects how we are perceived by others, which influences their reactions to us. Having a sense of style, to an extent, controls this outcome. Since control is an important principle of testosterone, it's wise to give attention to even these small details.

One way to demonstrate your respect for yourself is a shoe shine ... a slight effort which has a significant impact.

Men and jewelry don't mix.

―――

Spend the extra cash and buy better shoes.

―――

Black clothing is the most flattering.

―――

A man who doesn't take care of his shoes probably doesn't do a good job of wiping his ass.

Handwritten notes and letters still make an impact, particularly in this digital world we live in. This is a stamp I have for letters, with my name spelled in Chinese. You have to admit, it's classy.

Bowties should only be worn at weddings and balls,
but even that's too much.

A beard is alright,
but nothing beats a clean shave.

Never underestimate the value of a good haircut.

Vanity is for women. Save the hair dye for them.

Given options, go with wool.
Gabardine is best for suits and slacks.

If you must choose,
navy blue is the best color choice for a suit.

Mirrored sunglasses hide more than your eyes.

I live near the beach. These are my mirrored sunglasses. I've been wearing pairs like these since my lifeguarding days. They're very effective in more ways than one.

Rock gardens are the best bet—
they require no work and nothing dies.

Own a Zippo lighter.

When it comes to hats,
a Stetson stands out against all others.

The best sunglasses are polarized.

Men shouldn't wear cologne.
A man wasn't designed to smell like a woman.

Shenanigans

Fun and Games

One of the things that differentiated my late friend Roger Herring from other pals was his unending quest for fun. His never ceased, which made the time spent in his company memorable in so many ways. My brother, Bob, was known as "the king of fun and games" in college. He had already mastered most games, and he loved demonstrating his mastery over all comers. Games age, but they never grow old. Fun is fun. Both have a permanent place in the world of testosterone.

Never let the truth get in the way of a good story.

A good cigar isn't always an expensive cigar.

Commit to memory a few good clean jokes.

Memories don't last forever,
but photographs bring them to life.

Schedule some time to relax.
At times, it pays to have nothing to do.

All work and no play makes Jack a dull boy.

When you are a young boy, there are very few things more fun
than Scouting. Help the Scouts.

Gambling forgets history. Never forget history.

Try to enjoy yourself like today is the last day of your life,
as it may be. Life is far too fleeting.

When it rains, become counterintuitive;
pick up your head, raise your face, and enjoy the shower.

You really do need to know when to fold 'em.

Support wildlife, and throw a party every once in a while.

Don't live planning to leave your money to your heirs.

Pick the longest drink line,
it's the best place to make new friends.

Games are great intellectual stimulation. If you haven't tried chess, you're missing out. You get to focus on two opponents—whomever you play and yourself.

The most important move in chess is all of them.

Two illustrative words to describe retirement—"medical marijuana."

It has been my experience that folks who have no vices have very few virtues.
ABRAHAM LINCOLN

Don't bet the favorite to win, bet it to show.

It is better to lose a bet than to never place one at all.

Pay more attention to the cards being played
than to the person playing them.

Save your dart throwing for the pub.

It pays to cheat in drinking games.

Pornography is a waste of time.

Competition and Sports

Nothing riles a man's testosterone like competition and sports. Sports allow us to have fun while facing adversity and challenge. They bring out the best in us through repetition, resilience, and muscle memory. Best of all, they provide us opportunities to fight alongside other men while developing and perfecting our character.

For thirty-five years, I have been able to play in some incredible rugby competitions, with and against national and international players. My teammates and opponents have made these experiences unforgettable. Rugby has been the most significant experience in my life and I recommend it highly.

Having had the honor of playing hundreds of golf courses, one of the most memorable was The Mid Ocean Club in Bermuda, where Eisenhower and Churchill used to share a round.

Take a kid to a ballgame.

A hitter's perfection consists of failing
only sixty percent of the time.
GEORGE F. WILL IN "BUNTS"

A strong fastball is more effective and consistent
than a curveball.

Crowding the plate doesn't help you hit the ball.

I never set out to hurt anybody,
unless it was important, like a league game.
DICK BUTKUS

Give blood, play rugby. You'll be glad you did.

Pass the ball.

It's not whether you get knocked down,
it's whether you get up.
VINCE LOMBARDI

In sports, always run out the play.

Being average means you are just as close
to the bottom as you are to the top.
JOHN WOODEN

Pace makes the race.

In case you need an educated opinion, Sammy Baugh was the greatest football player of all time.

Give me scratching, diving, hungry ballplayers who come to kill you.
Leo Durocher

The best seat in a baseball park is down the third baseline. Second choice is behind home plate.

This Sam Snead Top Notch persimmon 4-wood has been in my bag since I started playing golf in high school.

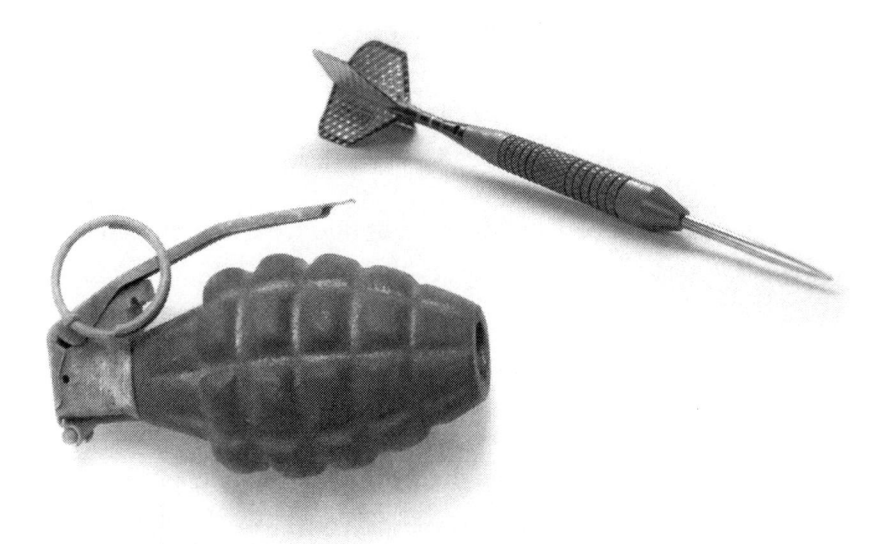

From throwing darts to throwing hand grenades, your performance will always improve when you invest time in practice.

Close only counts in horseshoes and hand grenades.

The grand slam is the most exciting play in baseball, followed by the triple.
Home runs happen all the time.

Unless you're a pro,
don't take yourself seriously on the golf course.

The main thing to do is relax and let your talent do the work.
CHARLES BARKLEY

You can't score if you don't take some shots.

Contact sports build character.

Drive for show, putt for dough.

In sports,
your offense will fail if you don't play solid defense.

Second place is for first losers.

Show me a good loser, and I'll show you a loser.
VINCE LOMBARDI

It's alright to collect trophies, just don't overdo it.

To the victor go the spoils.

It you want more wins, don't forget your losses.

It takes throwing a few gutter balls
to consistently throw strikes.

Vince Lombardi was the greatest football coach.

Compete hard at whatever you do and whenever you do it.

Animals and Nature

The natural world creates for us the opportunity to achieve our optimal testosterone level. Introducing animals into the equation provides gratification and makes bliss possible. Our enjoyment has no bounds when God's creation is the backdrop.

A dog is man's best friend.

Words cannot describe the joy and love my dogs provide me. This is Buck, our late Golden Retriever, getting ready for one of our outdoor adventures. My friends said he was more interesting than most people they'd met.

Animals are without sin. They deserve our respect.

Never mistreat an animal.

A mutt makes a very fine dog indeed.

Make sure your dog knows you're the boss,
but train it with much love.

The closer you stand to a horse
the more control you have.

The reason your dog drinks out of your toilet
is its water is usually fresh and cool.
That's the way you should keep their water bowl.

Lightning does strike twice.

The tree is a widow maker.
If you need to take one down,
it is very advisable to get chainsaw instruction in advance.

The North Star is the big star in line with the two stars
at the end of the Big Dipper's handle.

Plant early; it's much better than planting late.

When birds fly high they indicate good weather.

Everyone needs a monkey mask!

You'll get more out of climbing a tree
than just a better view.

If a tree falls in the woods, and nobody is around,
it still makes a sound.

The most beautiful country in the world is New Zealand.

There is no such thing as bad weather,
only the wrong type of clothing.

Never stand behind a horse.

Surf's up—somewhere.

Living and Loving

Life is too short, and it's full of surprises. Love is the wonderful essence of perfection—the orientation toward others. We can make plans for how we want our lives to unfold, but those plans won't unfold as scripted. These truths are more exacerbated with testosterone, because men are strivers by nature and conditioned to always seek the preferred result. Goals are good, but don't sweat the result. Just work hard, live your life to the fullest, love others, and leave the rest to God. The sooner a man learns he's not in charge, the earlier he gets to sit back and enjoy the ride.

> Only the heart knows how to find what is precious.
> FYODOR DOSTOYEVSKY

These are some pages from one of my father's many passports. He traveled widely all over the world. Its pages reflect a life fully lived. Travel is extremely fulfilling.

There really is a rat race,
so don't allow yourself to get caught up in it.

In chess, as in life, the pawn is usually moved first.

Your destination is where you are today.
The past is the past, so move on down the road.

It's usually a good thing to be your father's son.

You can't always get what you want.
THE ROLLING STONES
No truer words may ever have been sung (or spoken).

Emotions can get in the way of rational thinking.
Keep a clear head at all times.

Focus on where you are, rather than where you're going.
That way, you'll get to where you need to go.

In life, as in plumbing, it all flows downhill.

Nothing is fair. Fair is where they judge livestock.

It's a fool that looks for logic
in the chambers of the human heart.
O BROTHER, WHERE ART THOU?

This is an envelope of a letter my father wrote my grandmother soon after the attack on Pearl Harbor, which he had survived. He wrote his mother almost every day during his long and painful ride through the war in the Pacific. His commitment and love for his life back home helped him through that long war and made his life more meaningful to everyone else as well.

Love does not force its will on anyone.

Expect the real world to not always cooperate.

Do right and fear no man.

Self-pity ignores the world around it.

All that needs to be done for evil to exist
is for a few good men to do nothing.
SAINT AUGUSTINE

There are two things to never lend a friend:
your wife and your chainsaw.

The law of unintended consequences teaches that there are outcomes which are not intended.

Don't spend any time worrying about your enemies.

As you move through life, you're going to meet a few worms ... be prepared.

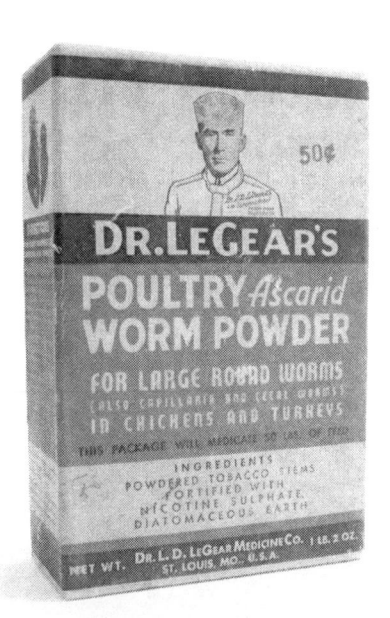

This is some recognition my father received from some of his buddies at work. Nothing means more than recognition amongst peers.

People

People always make life more interesting. Whether family, friends, or mere acquaintances, they can be the most wonderful parts of our lives or they can be a royal pain in the ass. Whatever the case, testosterone deals with others on its own terms. Even so, it's always helpful to consider the nitty-gritty; man has a sinful nature. Most behaviors are predictably consistent, and, complicating matters, everyone's unique. No doubt, people make the world a lot more interesting.

The legacy of heroes is the memory of a great name
and the inheritance of a great example.
BENJAMIN DISRAELI

Never underestimate the power of a snook.
BORIS FROM *THE ROCKY AND BULLWINKLE SHOW*

An incorrigible child should never be tolerated.
Time-out works wonders.

It is better to be alone than in bad company.
GEORGE WASHINGTON

The first thing we do, let's kill all the lawyers.
SHAKESPEARE

Be yourself.
No one else can do your part as well as you.

A man has to be what he is, Joey.
Alan Ladd in *Shane*

———

You can tell who someone is by looking at their friends.

———

Don't let anyone else design your life—that's your job.

———

All men seek autonomy.

There is a time and place for everything. Sometimes, it's just time to chill. Ain't nothin' too bad a little chillin' couldn't bear.

Go your own way.
Never try to be anyone but yourself.

No matter how poorly you do it,
sing your song.

There's many a good tune played on an old fiddle.

Tigers don't change their stripes—
neither do people.

Loyalty is based on memory.

Leave chemistry to the chemists—or a bartender.

Just like an iceberg,
there is usually much more beneath the surface.

Everyone should try to live out a few of their fantasies. Here is a reenactment of sorts with Bob House, Steve Homza, and Blair Fackler. As I said, I believe in a lot of ammo—it doesn't hurt to have good backup either.

>He that is good for making excuses
>is seldom good for anything else.
>BENJAMIN FRANKLIN

>Spare the rod, spoil the child.
>Said another way; when you eliminate discipline,
>you will likely spoil the child.
>Be gentle, but firm and consistent.

>You can't learn stupid.

If you're in Mexico and you're not a Mexican,
you're a gringo.

Not all of our personal characteristics are positive,
and not all human instincts are helpful;
therefore, it is important to understand oneself,
because it is difficult to overcome our nature.

Men, like bullets, go farther when polished.

Don't wait for a lifeboat
to put women and children first.

Bad habits can be tolerable
when they're your own.

Exercise and Health

Men and their testosterone will be squandered when not fully utilized. Each of us needs to be ready to perform physically at a moment's notice, and that takes discipline and commitment. Exercise sucks, but the lack of it is much worse. One of our great blessings is our health. We must never take it for granted.

Don't ever use a treadmill.
When you age, your knees are likely going to be
the first thing that fails you.

You can never consume enough water.

Your fitness is critical.

One in six men will be diagnosed with prostate cancer.
The exam isn't fun,
but the odds make the exam worth the pain.

Your liver is your lifeline, so every once and a while,
give it a rest.

Carnivores need to eat plants too.
Don't forget to eat plenty of fruit and vegetables.

It is far better to skip a meal than a workout.
Far too many never miss a meal and work out sporadically.

Exercise is medicine.

Floss, as your teeth need all the help they can get.

A drunken man usually deserves whatever is coming.

Muscle mass is the first thing to go as you age,
and it quickly weakens without repetition.
Weight training later in life is critical.

Exercise is more effective when rest follows it.

Smoking kills.

There are no gains without pain.
FROM BENJAMIN FRANKLIN

Pain is weakness leaving the body.

Nothing turns on a woman more than firm abs.
Sorry.

When you weight train,
use mostly dumbbells.
You will like your results.

Work and Labor

For men, manual labor is inevitable, and testosterone never shies away from things that take energy and effort. That is why real men have it in such a lopsided dose. Never waste it. We are built to put ourselves to good use.

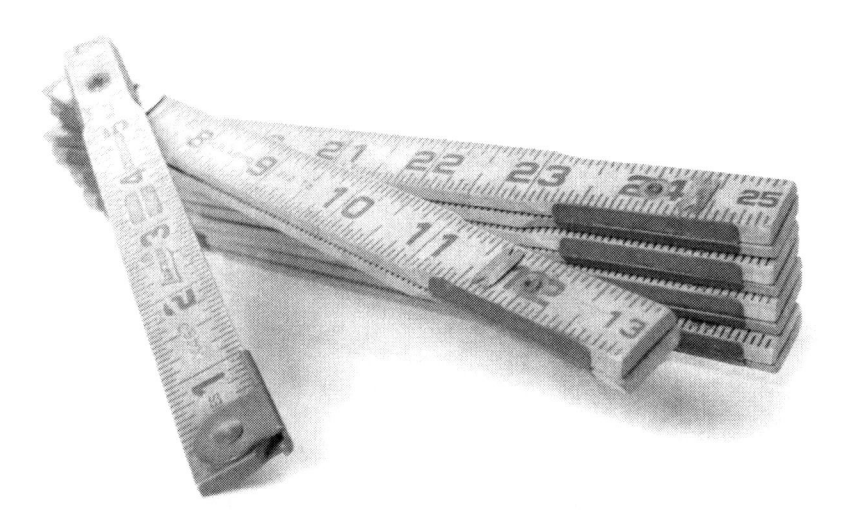

You can use some tools so often they become an extension of your personality. I have had this expandable carpenter's ruler since shop class in junior high school.

Hardware stores are always good for entertainment.

Let the saw do the work.

A can of WD-40 belongs in every toolbox.

Always dilute bleach.

Duct tape should be in every toolbox.

If you can't break a bolt loose, apply heat.

It's great to be a jack of all trades,
but even better to be the master of at least one.

Leather gloves can make you and your tools
more effective.

Solid wheels on wheelbarrows, wagons, and dollies
are always preferable.

The right tool makes even hard tasks much easier.

Cut once, measure twice.

We have a lot of fun out in my bar having people guess what certain tools are. Here is an item that usually stumps a lot of people—a beehive smoker.

Vise-grips belong in every toolbox.

Drop-shipping is aptly named.

House gutters are high maintenance
and usually unnecessary.

There is no such thing as cheap paint.
If it's cheap, it isn't paint.

Vaseline is great for protecting metal from rust.

When digging with a spade or shovel, take small bites.
That way you'll double your efficiency.

When you're finished using tools,
always return them to the place where you found them.

With gas fittings,
remember it's the opposite of "righty tighty, lefty loosey."

Gentlemen and Hacks

Religion and the Arts

Testosterone thrives under the watchful eye of a loving God, yet it can be warped by religious dogma. Art is much the same. It is all around us, yet it's routinely diminished by self-appointed experts.

Beware of the pious man.

The only church key I've ever needed.

Forget poetry.

It is never too late to read the Classics.

I long for the time when the last king would be strangled
by the entrails of the last priest.
THOMAS JEFFERSON

Culture, whatever it is, is overrated.

This is a self-portrait sculpture given as a gift to me by the artist. A humble man, he will remain anonymous, although his name is listed in this book's Acknowledgments. His favorite line: "It's all bullshit."

Shakespeare is worthwhile,
even though Tolstoy would disagree.

The vast majority of poetry is worthless—
unless you're the writer.

There is nothing wrong with Hollywood
that a lot of funerals won't solve.

Politics and Government

There is little difference between politicians, and their ineptitude is predictable and practically universal. Political parties further muddy the situation. Testosterone ferrets through it all fairly easily because it doesn't tolerate ambiguity. It pays attention to what politicians get done and little else. Nearly all candidates for office patronize voting blocs, are not candid, and are habitually hypocritical when they talk about their opponents. What we need in government is more testosterone.

This is a piece of the Berlin Wall. It was given to me by a CIA agent who was there when the wall was pulled down. It provides a constant reminder of what governments are capable of when they work to stifle freedom.

> That government is best which governs least.
> HENRY DAVID THOREAU

Things are usually a lot more simple—or complicated—than politicians make them out to be.

Beware of blind dates and government.
In both cases, you don't know what you're dealing with.

Socialism is for pussies.

Freedom is never more than one generation
away from extinction.
RONALD REAGAN

Our liberty is ensured by four boxes:
the ballot box, the jury box,
the soapbox, and the cartridge box.

One must bear in mind that the expansion of
federal activity is a form of eating for politicians.
WILLIAM F. BUCKLEY, JR.

Deficits allow our representatives to vote for spending without
having to vote taxes to pay for it,
and that creates irresponsibility.
MILTON FRIEDMAN

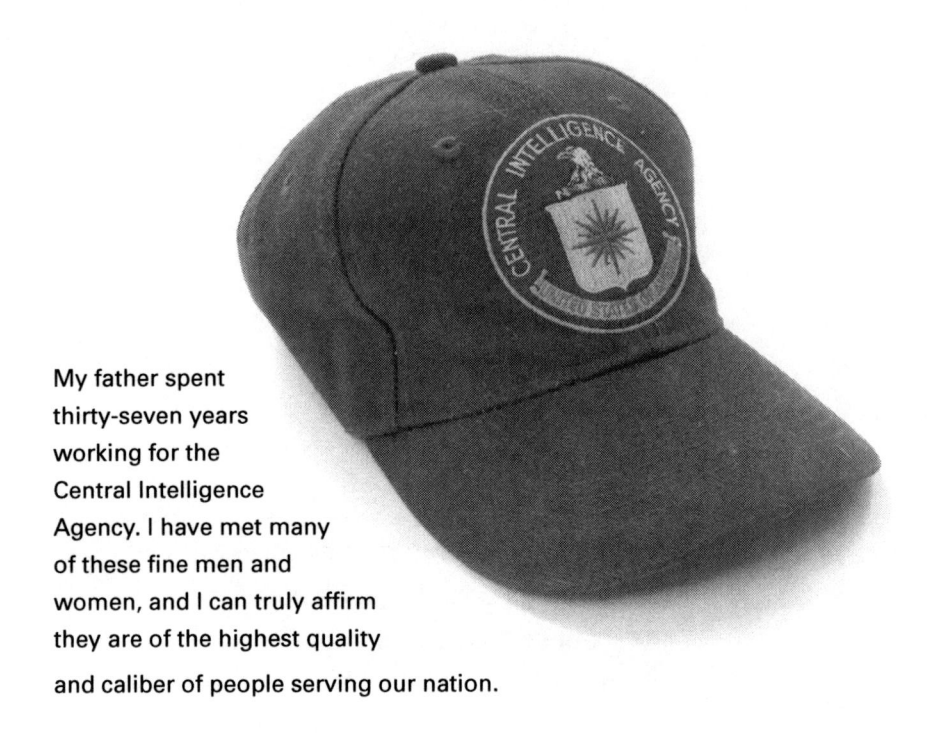

My father spent thirty-seven years working for the Central Intelligence Agency. I have met many of these fine men and women, and I can truly affirm they are of the highest quality and caliber of people serving our nation.

> The people never give up their liberties
> but under some delusion.
> EDMUND BURKE

A libertarian wants the government
to leave everyone alone and let everyone be,
which is too unambiguous a policy for most politicians.

Those who would give up essential Liberty, to purchase a little
temporary Safety, deserve neither Liberty nor Safety.
BENJAMIN FRANKLIN

A well regulated Militia,
being necessary to the security of a free State,
the right of the people to keep and bear arms,
shall not be infringed.
AMENDMENT II:
THE CONSTITUTION OF THE UNITED STATES

Is life so dear or peace so sweet
as to be purchased at the price of chains and slavery?
Forbid it, Almighty God!
I know not what course others may take,
but as for me, give me liberty, or give me death.
PATRICK HENRY

Politicians all have an agenda.
Make sure you know it before you give them your vote.

Business

In business, most management types, analysts, and consultants act like the solutions to most problems are clear and simple. They're not; just ask the front-line workers. Most solutions take time and energy to implement, even when they're straightforward. Injecting a little testosterone in the workplace can really make an astonishing difference.

This is the barometer in my study. I take a keen interest in the weather, and I monitor details that help me make weather-related decisions. I do the same in business; it pays to keep an eye on measurements that give you a clear picture of performance and results.

Most mistakes are not fatal.

The best predictor of future behavior is past behavior.

The further up the organizational ladder you go,
the further away from the truth you get.

Those that spend too much time thinking in the long-term,
get fired in the short-term.

JACK ROSS

Nothing ventured, nothing gained.

Only the paranoid survive.
ANDY GROVE, FORMER INTEL CEO

Urgency speeds up results.
At the end of WWII, it only took the Germans eighty-nine days to develop a jet engine.

Proper planning and preparation prevents piss-poor performance.
BRITISH ARMY ADAGE

If it's important, put it in writing.

Don't lend money, unless you think you're a bank.

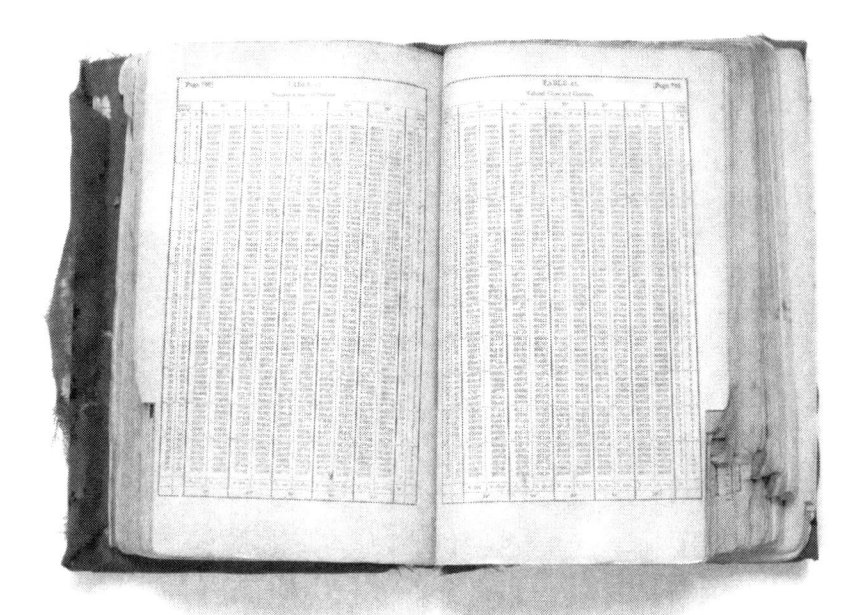

This was one of my grandfather's books, and as a captain in the Merchant Marine, books were the tools of his trade—the Azimuths of the Sun, Time at Ship, and his Latitude and Longitude Tables. For me, they are a business metaphor, maintaining all the relevant and important information you need ready and at your fingertips. Understanding and being prepared with the facts will always serve you well.

It's alright to say you don't know.

Business is business, it's not personal.

AN ADAPTATION FROM *THE GODFATHER*

Anybody can be a success for a day.

Give people the benefit of the doubt—
until you know them better.

If it's stupid, but works, it isn't stupid.

Deal with passive-aggressive behavior in others forcefully,
as you now know how weak they really are.

Symbols are important.

Making lists helps.
You don't have a personal reminder service—
unless you're married.

Never look like you're working.

You get what you pay for, and remember,
the contract usually goes to the lowest bidder.

Speak the truth, and whenever possible, speak your mind.

A verbal contract isn't worth the paper it's written on.
Sam Goldwyn

It pays to be skeptical of upper management.

Lawyers don't run the world, accountants do.

Put yourself in a position to say "yes"
more than you say "no."

Never avoid taking responsibility,
unless someone else is responsible.

This is one of several briefcases I own. I used to take them home with me a lot and attempt to get work done after hours. However, I never found that it really made much of a difference. Now, I do whatever I can to complete my work during regular working hours. My sanity has improved greatly.

The best job is one with lots of days off.

After all,
the chief business of the American people is business.
CALVIN COOLIDGE

Titles aren't important,
just ask a sanitation engineer.

Buy low, sell high.

There are no downsides to teamwork.

When you find yourself juggling a lot of balls,
make sure you don't let the big ones drop.

Don't always follow the money.

Imagination is worth more with a little restraint.

Don't rest on your laurels.

Our family has had military roots going back generations. That is my great-great-grandfather, fourth from the left.

The Military

I'm sure it wasn't because my testosterone germinated eight miles south of the Pentagon, but I did wonder why my Marine father would conduct almost daily inspections of my bedroom. I never needed the chain of command explained to me. After I graduated from a Department of Defense high school overseas, my father spent more time discussing the military lifestyle. Even though I never served, my father's and grandfather's respect for the military is deeply instilled in me.

Gentle when stroked, fierce when provoked.
THE MOTTO OF THE FIGHTING 69TH

———

Loose lips sink ships.

———

There are no atheists in a foxhole.
CAPTAIN JAMES LAWRENCE

———

In war there can be no substitute for victory.
GENERAL DOUGLAS MACARTHUR

———

A draft dodger isn't worth a bucket of warm spit.

———

Don't give up the ship.

———

If the enemy is in range, so are you.

Here is my father at age seventeen, just out of Marine Corps boot camp in Parris Island, S.C. When my son went there for boot camp, he had this picture placed in his hat. I have never been so moved by a gesture.

There is no little enemy.
BENJAMIN FRANKLIN

The point of attack may need to be more than one point.

Victory does not mean winning battles,
it means winning the war.

Avoid engagement with a superior force.

Five-second fuses last about three seconds.
INFANTRY JOURNAL

The object of war is not to die for your country,
but to make the other bastard die for his.
GENERAL GEORGE S. PATTON

In case you didn't notice, there is a global jihad going on.
Don't allow yourself or others to forget about it.

"The whole nine yards" doesn't refer to football.
It's the length of the ammunition belt in a P-51 Mustang.

An army of sheep led by a lion is better than
an army of lions led by a sheep.
ATTRIBUTED TO ALEXANDER THE GREAT

Always support the troops,
and never forget the wounded.

Being Awake When it Matters

Intelligence and Learning

Intelligence isn't about IQ. Your IQ, or intelligence quotient, simply means the aptitude you have to learn. It isn't a measure of the knowledge one already possesses.

Some guys are exposed to a few things, yet ignore or disregard what they are told or taught. Not so with a man of testosterone. He knows better, already realizing the painfully obvious—he doesn't have all the answers. In humility, he defers to his role models.

Here I am at Camp Shenandoah with Norfolk's Troop #1, with my son and friend Bob Heely and his son Ted. A young man learns invaluable life lessons by following the Scout credo—A Scout is: Trustworthy, Loyal, Helpful, Friendly, Courteous, Kind, Obedient, Cheerful, Thrifty, Brave, Clean, Reverent.

> The difference between stupidity and genius
> is that genius has its limits.
> ALBERT EINSTEIN

> Too many people see what they want to see,
> and think what they want to think,
> regardless of the evidence.

Independent thinking leads to wisdom and fairness.

Not all that you learn is good.

You don't have to lift the lid to smell what's cooking.

The art of being wise is knowing what to overlook.
WILLIAM JAMES

Contentment isn't hard to attain—it's just hard to realize.

If you get used to something,
it's likely time to quit.

Memories are selective.
It is important not to forget that.

Discernment is learned through practice.

An irrational person
won't be persuaded by a rational argument.

Only a fool is ignorant of history.

Not too many good things happen
on the street late at night.

Reading is the best thing you can undertake
to improve yourself. Learning matters.

It is valuable to imagine what the world looks like
through someone else's eyes.

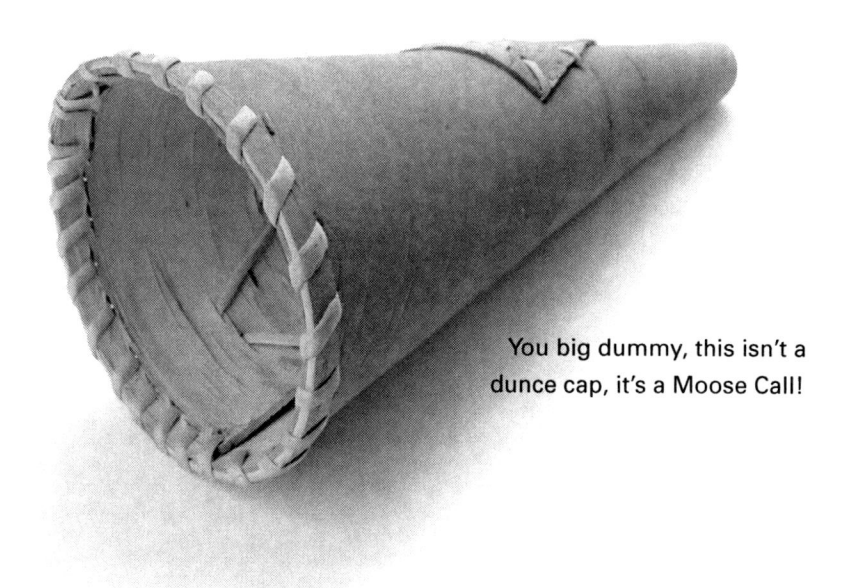

You big dummy, this isn't a dunce cap, it's a Moose Call!

The world is full of amateurs.

The great disturbing factor in a man's life
is ignorance of good and evil.
CICERO

Language is caught, not taught.

An unarmed man
doesn't stand a chance in a battle of wits.

The finest testosterone education is absorbed best around a campfire.

Don't overestimate the worth of a formal education. Highly educated people do stupid things all the time.

If you know too much, you'll get old too soon.

You can't judge a book by its cover.

No one has ever understood the nature of the human condition, so don't try to be the first.

———

Read the Book of Ecclesiastes; its author, Solomon, was the wisest man to walk the earth.

———

You can teach an old dog new tricks.

———

The true creator is necessity,
who is the mother of our invention.
PLATO

———

Necessity is the mother of all invention.
ALBERT EINSTEIN

———

No one gets wise from another's woe.

Watch your step. Horseshit is everywhere you turn.

There is no education like the second kick of a mule.

Perfection is the enemy of progress.

The opinion pages of a newspaper
have the least value in the product.

There's a sucker born every minute.

What you learn after you graduate is what really matters.

There are dumb-asses wherever you turn.

SURVIVAL

Testosterone is always ready for a worst-case scenario. Sometimes it comes down to preparation and prayer. Roger Bannister, the first man to run a mile in under four minutes, explains survival:

"Every morning in Africa, a gazelle wakes up. It knows it must outrun the fastest lion or it will be killed. Every morning in Africa, a lion wakes up. It knows it must run faster than the slowest gazelle, or it will starve. It doesn't matter whether you're a lion or a gazelle—when the sun comes up, you'd better be running."

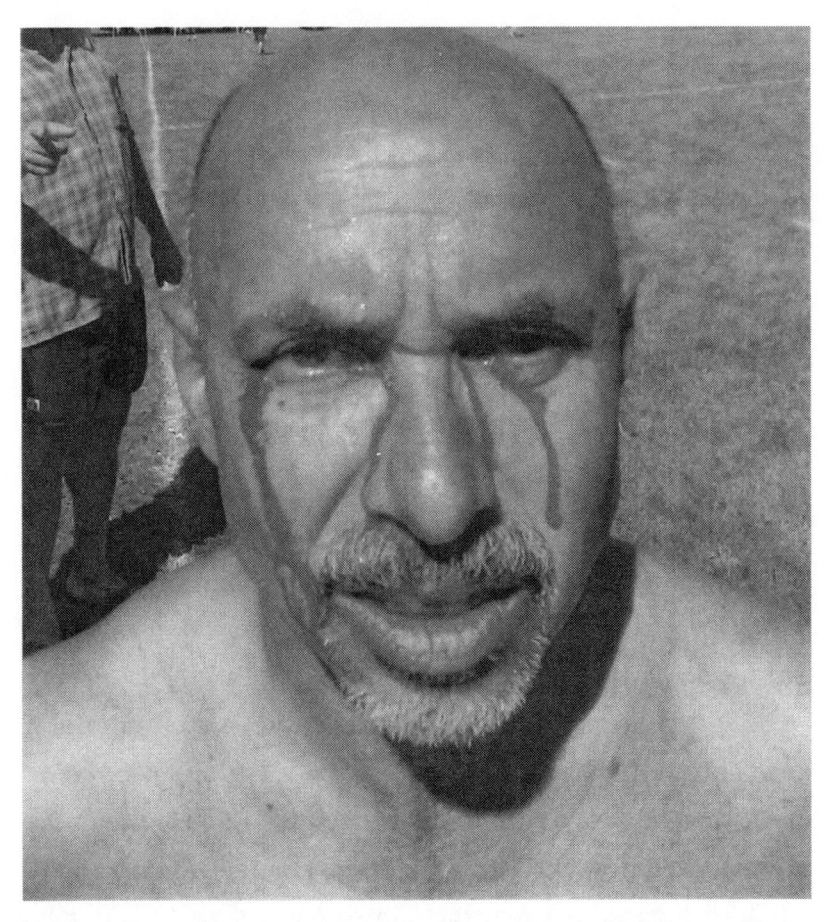

Rugby is the only game that celebrates the survival of its players. Here is Mike Bressi, a real man of testosterone, after a recent game. Who needs stitches when someone has a camera?

Don't try to swim against the current.

A good lawyer knows the law,
a great lawyer knows the judge.

Always carry your folding money in your front pocket.
No one will take it without your knowledge.

File a flight plan, even when you're not flying.

"Fire in the hole" means pay attention.

Always lock your doors.

Back in your vehicle whenever possible.
You never know when you'll need to make a quick exit.

Cut, stack, and cover your wood in the spring.

Even when your plan is solid,
don't underestimate the value of a backup plan.

———

Keep a flashlight in every vehicle's glove box.

———

Trick me once, shame on you;
trick me twice, shame on me.

———

Get good directions before you leave.
You won't want to stop and ask for them later.

———

Make sure you know who packed your parachute.

———

Make sure you get a second opinion—
and at least three bids.

Master the art of treading water.
It beats the alternative.

Sit with your back to the wall.

There really is such a thing as survival of the fittest,
and remember, there is also a food chain.

Studying your map before the trip
will help you read it later.

It's not what you're going through,
it's how you go through it.

Plan your escape route well before your need to escape.

Leadership

Just managing things will never suffice for testosterone. Leadership is what testosterone calls for, and leadership is influencing events and others. If you're not swaying what's going on, then you're not leading anything or anyone. Testosterone demands impact.

Actions speak louder than words, and results are what matter. After the first thirty years of Norfolk Blues Rugby, our record was 480-176-11.

All for one, one for all.
THE THREE MUSKETEERS, ALEXANDRE DUMAS

———

Confidence shouldn't be overdone or underrated.

———

Nothing ventured, nothing gained.

Know your stuff, be a man, look after your men.
  DOUGLAS SOUTHALL FREEMAN

———

All leadership is other-oriented.

———

Confidence is important,
but showing confidence in others is more important.

———

Don't fear authority, just respect it.

———

Don't preach a sermon you can't follow yourself.

———

Give advice reluctantly.

———

It pays to allow oneself to be persuaded by the facts.

Just because you have some bad news
doesn't mean you shouldn't share it.

Just because you know the problem
doesn't mean you're closer to fixing it.

Lead, follow, or get out of the way.
THOMAS PAINE

The quickest way to fail is to try
to please everybody.

This is one of my grandfather's U.S. Navy Civil War cutlasses and was used when he commissioned several ships during WWII. Of note, a cutlass isn't traditionally an officer's sword. My grandfather was proud he came up the hard way.

The view only changes for the lead dog.
Sergeant Preston of The Yukon

It's not what you earn, it's what you give.

React to bad news quickly, and in person.

You attract more flies with honey.

A decision not to make a decision
is many times the preferred decision.

The higher you climb, the colder it gets.

Reality

Testosterone is pragmatic. It only deals with facts. It has no room for conjecture and prejudice. It won't prejudge anything. It also won't ignore anything. It's honest. Ignorance is blindness. Testosterone is real; it's reality.

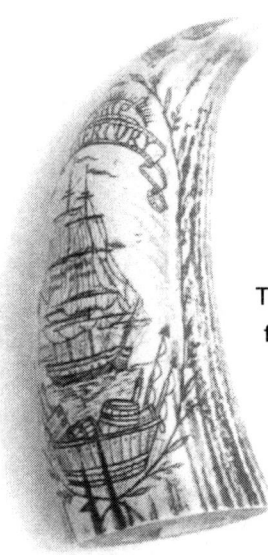

This is a piece of scrimshaw I own. Not really. It's a fake. I'm glad, because I don't believe we should harvest bones for art. It also reminds me that what you see isn't always real, or the truth.

Yesterday doesn't determine tomorrow.

If you hang out at a barbershop long enough, you're going to get a haircut.

Contact with real life will cure most idealists. Unfortunately, too many people live in la-la land.

Some things really are forever.

History repeats itself.

There's never just one cockroach in the kitchen.

Crime doesn't pay.

Things that seem to be too good to be true usually are.

Opinions are like assholes—everyone's got one.

The world is a struggle between good and evil.

Even a blind squirrel finds a nut every once in a while.

There is no perfection in the human form.

These are some of my duck and goose calls. They're used to disguise myself as waterfowl. Seems like cheating. In the real world, there are a lot of birds out there cheating too.

Your sins will always find you.

Where there is smoke, there is fire.

It's usually never too late.

It is what it is.

It's a man's world.
Don't ever forget it.

ACKNOWLEDGMENTS

To the following men—these rugby brothers, hunting and fishing partners, teammates, golfers, drinking buddies, and friends, I thank you for your companionship.

You each have a place in *The Book of Testosterone*.

Adam Goldblatt	Bill Eisenbeiss
Adriaan Verheul	Bill Fink
Al Lucus	Bill Gardner
Alan Larivee	Bill Hayward
Alan Levenstein	Bill Johnson
Alex Kalasinsky	Bill Richardson
Alvin DeJesus	Bill Roark
Andy Creekmore	Bill Schneider
Andy Tysinger	Bill Shepherd
Anthony Bueno	Bill Van Buren
Ben Vanderberry	Bill Young
Bert Trojanowski	Billy Wilson
Bev Nash	Blair Fackler
Bill Blake	Blitz Antlitz
Bill Brownley	Bob Carswell
Bill Campbell	Bob Cowin
Bill Cresenzo	Bob Good
Bill Deany	Bob Hames
Bill Dickie	Bob Heely

Bob Herron	Chris Neikirk
Bob House	Chris Petrakes
Bob Linsley	Chris Porter
Bob Lynn	Chuck Chrisostomo
Bob Marcus	Clay Culbreth
Bob Molinaro	Clyde Holzer
Bob Morgan	Cole Fackler
Bob Williamson	Collin Crawford
Bobby Gebron	Conny Roussos
Brack Fischer	Conrad Hall
Brad Fisher	Courtney Evans
Brad Mills	Curt Hacker
Brad Overton	Curt Herron
Brandon Kolipano	Curtis Hall
Brant Lewis	Cutch Armstrong
Brian Cooper	Dale Bowen
Brian Vizard	Dale Carlson
Brice Maccubbin	Dan O'Connell
Bruce Bradley	Dan Roach
Bruce Marcus	Dan Santoro
Bruce Pepper	Dan Sykes
Bruce Rader	Dane Cheek
Bubba Cochrane	Danny Lonergan
Buster Laurenson	Danny McGrain
Carl Ostermann	Dave Chapman
Cary Kennedy	Dave Culler
Cecil Achord	Dave Hamberg
Charles Barker	Dave Holley
Charlie Carlson	Dave Iwans
Charlie Hill	Dave Mele
Chris Knight	Dave Reno
Charlie Stitzer	Dave Stearns
Chic Kelty	Dayle Runner
Chilly Kirkwood	Demetrio Cardiel
Chip Fenn	Denis Finley
Chip Gilbert	Dennis Ellmer
Chris Adams	Dennis Hartig
Chris Blount	Dennis See
Chris Branum	Dennis Stoneman

Dennis Williams	George Butts
Denny Morgan	George Fiscella
Dick Greene	George Harr
Dick Unger	George Johnson
Dimetri Hionis	George Little
Don Bilbo	George Mirmelstein
Don Mastaccio	George Wilder
Don Tracy	Gerry Reust
Doug Haupt	Gil McMillan
Drake Van de Castle	Glenn Miller
Drew Little	Gordie Shuman
Drew Rosen	Greg Jordan
Drew Savage	Greg Robinette
Duffy Drum	Greg Spivak
Dwight Schaubach	Grey Persons
Ed Gafney	Gordon Borrell
Ed Heimer	Hal Hamberg
Ed Lewis	Harpo
Ed Logue	Hennie van Zyl
Ed Power	Henry Atterbury
Eddie Brooks	Henry Blaha
Eric Bird	Henry Posko
Eric Eller	Hillary Robinette
Eric Heinicke	Howard Steir
Eric Miller	Howard Tew
Eric Smith	Howie Chadborne
Fran Russell	J. C. Watts
Frank Batten	J.B. Blount
Frank Cullen	Jack Horn
Frank Gigliotti	Jack Ross
Frank Ryan	Jackson Stitzer
Fred Kirsch	James Crell
Fred Stinard	James Painter
Gary Lambert	Jamie Newnam
Gene Adams	Jamie Wright
Gene Jernigan	Jared Council
Gene Kostinas	Jason Owens
George Boothby	Jason Trimyer
George Brooks	Jay Herring

Jeff Anderson	John Fall
Jeff Bush	John Fenn
Jeff Paine	John Hutchinson
Jeff Sands	John Kamauff
Jerry Davis	John Kinsley
Jerry Gilfoyle	John Koehler
Jim Booker	John Lawrence
Jim Browning	John Muldoon
Jim Corzatt	John Owens
Jim Frohman	John Ridenour
Jim Howley	John Strope
Jim Moylan	Jim Thompson
Jim Rosato	John Tracy
Jim Tracy	John Via
Jim Troutman	John White
Jim Turner	John Wilcox
Jim Wallace	John Witte
Jimmy Bain	Johnny Bock
Jimmy Vita	Johnny "Ethan" Phillips
Joe Antle	Jon Knight
Joe Coccaro	Jon Wheeler
Joe DeLatte	Josh Kemp
Joe DePalma	Josh Moto
Joe Gaber	Keith Cassidy
Joe Kiley	Keith Dennis
Joe Mattingley	Keith Mclean
Joe Takach	Keith Wright
Joe Taranto	Ken Lees
Joey DePalma	Ken Myers
Johan Varverud	Ken Worm
John "Spice" Hamilton	Kenny McCombs
John "Sugar" Hamilton	Kevin Shwedo
John Carr	Kevin Will
John Dodson	Larry Richardson
John Donat	Larry Stark
John Donnellan	Lee Tolliver
John Doud	Lex Maccubbin
John Eales	Linwood Beckner
John Ellis	Louis Smith

Lundy Sykes	Mike Monaco
Marc Butler	Mike Old
Mario Zigeri	Mike Osborne
Mark Bennett	Mike Posko
Mark Benson	Mike Puopolo
Mark Keller	Mike Valentine
Mark Lambourne	Mike Ware
Mark Rasmussen	Mike Witter
Mark Smith	Mike Wright
Mark Steiner	Morgan Davis
Mark Willoughby	Nathan Drory
Marsh Pennington	Nelson Brown
Marty Edrich	Nelson DeCruz
Matt "Tatonka" Szkotak	Nic Mumejian
Matt Ellmer	Nick Vaselli
Matt Godek	Otis Purvis
Matt Leonard	Owen Griffin
Matt Robinette	Pat Patterson
Maurice Childers	Paul Myers
Maurice Jones	Paul Pate
Max Owens	Paul Shugrue
Michael Alston	Pedro Wildenburg
Michael Chu	Pete Freeman
Michael Hasty	Pete Lively
Michael Powers	Phil Dorsey
Mick Christ	Phil Kessler
Mike "Cajun" Bermes	Phil Lewis
Mike Abernathy	Phil Newswanger
Mike Braham	Phil Spayd
Mike Bressi	Porter Hardy
Mike D'Orso	Randy Hargrave
Mike Duman	Ray Payne
Mike Goldsmith	Reginald Tift
Mike Hamel	Ric Kempton
Mike Henrich	Ric McBride
Mike Hudson	Rich Etzkorn
Mike Ireland	Richard Morris
Mike Jeter	Rick Clanton
Mike Lambert	Rick Knapp

Rick Zubiate	Stephen Hanks
Rob Christian	Sterling Marshall
Rob Greenough	Steve Burgess
Rob Herring	Steve Cade
Rob Poehlnitz	Steve Homza
Robert Circelli	Steve Hough
Robert Davis	Steve McWhorter
Roger Herring	Steve O'Bara
Ron Black	Steve Potter
Ronny Herring	Steve Sakis
Ron Della Donne	Steve Tinkham
Ron Hurwitz	Steve Walters
Ron Murray	Steve Whitaker
Ronnie Maccubbins	Steven Graves
Ronnie Engleman	Steven Russell
Rory Lewis	Stuart Corker
Roy Manuel	Ted Colna
Russ Kostinas	Ted Drake
Rusty Friddell	Terry Cramm
Ryan Mulske	Terry Lee
Sam Kline	Terry O'Donnell
Sam Kowalski	Terry Whelan
Sam Smyth	Tim Dankanich
Sam Taylor	Tim Largen
Sandy Sands	Tim McGuire
Schyler Whelan	Tim Rayfield
Scott Cash	Tim Spruill
Scott Herring	Tim Trivett
Scott Mackey	Todd Musick
Scott Rigell	Tom Donovan
Scott Vance	Tom Duke
Scotty Norris	Tom Ivey
Sean Brickell	Tom Oxenham
Sean Whelan	Tom Rozier
Shawn Gannon	Tom Sarisky
Ski Miller	Tom Sourlis
Skip Yeager	Tom Townsend
Speedy Gainer	Tom Trumps
Stacy Cummings	Tom Watkins

Tom West
Tommy Baldwin
Tommy Butt
Tommy Drew
Tommy Kennan
Tommy Mayes
Tony Bird
Tony Bird, Jr.
Tony Brooks
Tony Cerza
Tony Martinette
Tony See
Tracy Burge
Trey Guion
Tucker Burns
Tyler Maccubbin
Vince Mastracco
Walter Reinhardt
Walter Wilkins
Wes Cummings
Will Crell
Will Thornton
Wilson Cocke
Wim Brown
Win Brooks

Submit your own quotes and photos

Go to www.thebookoftestosterone.com and follow the directions to add either your own quote, a great quote said by one of your favorite role models, or an unusual photo with a caption.